Laugh and Live

Laugh and Live

By
DOUGLAS FAIRBANKS

ILLUSTRATED

NEW YORK
BRITTON PUBLISHING COMPANY

TO MY MOTHER

CONTENTS

LIST OF ILLUSTRATIONS

———

LAUGH AND LIVE

CHAPTER I

"WHISTLE AND HOE—SING AS WE GO"

There is one thing in this good old world that is positively sure—happiness is for *all* who *strive* to *be* happy—and those who laugh *are* happy.

Everybody is eligible—you—me—the other fellow.

Happiness is fundamentally a state of mind—not a state of body.

And mind controls.

Indeed it is possible to stand with one foot on the inevitable "banana peel" of life with both eyes peering into the Great Beyond, and still be happy, comfortable, and serene—if we will even so much as smile.

It's all a state of mind, I tell you—and I'm sure of what I say. That's why I have taken

9

up my fountain pen. I want to talk to my friends
—you hosts of people who have written to me
for my recipe. In moving pictures all I can do
is act my part and grin for you. What I say is
a matter of your own inference, but with my pen
I have a means of getting around the "silent
drama" which prevents us from organizing a
"close-up" with one another.

In starting I'm going to ask you "foolish
question number 1."—

Do you ever laugh?

I mean do you ever laugh right out—spontan-
eously—just as if the police weren't listening
with drawn clubs and a finger on the button
connecting with the "hurry-up" wagon? Well,
if you don't, you should. *Start off the morning
with a laugh and you needn't worry about the rest
of the day.*

I like to laugh. It is a tonic. It braces me
up—makes me feel fine!—and keeps me in prime
mental condition. Laughter is a physiological
necessity. The nerve system requires it. The
deep, forceful chest movement in itself sets the

blood to racing thereby livening up the circulation—which is good for us. Perhaps you hadn't thought of that? Perhaps you didn't realize that laughing automatically re-oxygenates the blood —*your* blood—and keeps it red? It does all of that, and besides, it relieves the tension from your brain.

Laughter is more or less a habit. To some it comes only with practice. But what's to hinder practising? Laugh and live long—if you had a thought of dying—laugh and grow well— if you're sick and despondent—laugh and grow fat—if your tendency is towards the lean and cadaverous—laugh and succeed—if you're glum and "unlucky"—laugh and nothing can faze you —not even the Grim Reaper—for the man who has laughed his way through life has nothing to fear of the future. His conscience is clear.

Wherein lies this magic of laughter? For magic it is—a something that manufactures a state of felicity out of any condition. We've got to admit its charm; automatically and inevitably a laugh cheers us up. If we are bored—nothing to do—

just laugh—that's something to do, for laughter is synonymous with action, and action dispels gloom, care, trouble, worry and all else of the same ilk.

Real laughter is spontaneous. Like water from the spring it bubbles forth a creation of mingled action and spontaneity—two magic potions in themselves—the very essence of laughter —the unrestrained emotion within us!

So, for me, it is to laugh! Why not stick along? The experiment won't hurt you. All we need is will power, and that is a personal matter for each individual to seek and acquire for himself. Many of us already possess it, but many of us do not.

Take the average man on the street for example. Watch him go plodding along—no spring, no elasticity, no vim. He is in *check-rein*—how can he laugh when his *pep* is all gone and the *sand in his craw* isn't there any more? What he needs is *spirit!* Energy—the power to force himself into action! For him there is no hope unless he will take up physical training in some form that will put him in normal physical condition—after that everything simplifies itself. The brain responds to the new blood in circulation and thus the mental processes are ready to make a fight against the inertia of stagnation which has held them in bondage.

And, mind you, physical training doesn't necessarily mean going to an expert for advice. One doesn't have to make a mountain out of a molehill. Get out in the fresh air and walk briskly—and don't forget to wear a smile while you're at it. Don't over-do. Take it easy at first and build on your effort day by day. A little this morning —a little more tonight. The first chance you have, when you're sure of your wind and heart, get out upon the country road, or cross-country hill and dale. Then run, run, run, until you drop exhausted upon some grassy bank. Then laugh, loud and long, for you're on the road to happiness.

Try it now—don't wait. *Today is the day to begin*. Or, if it is night when you run across these lines, drop this book and trot yourself around the block a few times. Then come back and you'll enjoy it more than you would otherwise. Activity makes for happiness as nothing else will and once you stir your blood into little bubbles of energy you will begin to think of other means of keeping your bodily house in order. Unless you make a first effort the chances are you will do very little real thinking of any kind—*we need pep to think*.

Think what an opportunity we miss when stripped at night if we fail to give our bodies a round of exercise. It is so simple, so easy, and has so much to do with our sleep each night and our work next day that to neglect to do so is a crime against nature. And laugh! Man alive, if you are not in the habit of laughing, *get the habit*. Never miss a chance to laugh aloud. Smiling is better than nothing, and a chuckle is better still—but *out and out laughter* is the real thing. Try it now if you dare! And when you've done it, analyze your feelings.

I make this prediction—if you once start the habit of exercise, and couple with it the habit

White Studio

Do You Ever Laugh?

of laughter, even if only for one short week—
you'll keep it up ever afterwards.

And, by the way, Friend Reader,—don't be
alarmed. The personal pronouns *"I"* and *"you"*
give place in succeeding chapters to the more con-
genial editorial *"we."* I couldn't resist the temptation to enjoy one brief spell of intimacy just
for the sake of good acquaintance. *Have a laugh
on me.*

CHAPTER II

Experience is the real teacher, but the matter of how we are going to succeed in life should not be left to ordinary chance while we are waiting for things to happen. Our first duty is to prepare ourselves against untoward experiences, and that is best done by taking stock of our mental and physical assets at the very outset of our journey. What weaknesses we possess are excess baggage to be thrown away and that is our reason for taking stock so early. It is likely to save us from riding to a fall.

There is one thing we don't want along—*fear*. We will never get anywhere with that, nor with any of its uncles, aunts or cousins—*Envy, Malice and Greed*. In justice to our own best interests we should search every crook and cranny of our hearts and minds lest we venture forth with any such impedimenta. There is no excuse, and we have no one to blame if we allow any of them to journey along with us. We know whether they are there or not just as we would know *Courage, Trust and Honor* were they perched behind us on the saddle.

It is idle to squeal if through association with the former we find ourselves ditched before we are well under way—for it is coming to us, sooner or later. We might go *far,* as some have done, through the lanes and alleys of ill-gotten gains and luxurious self-indulgence, but we would pay in the end. So, why not charge them up to "profit and loss" at the start and kick them off into the gutter where they belong? They are not for us on our eventful journey through life, and the time to get rid of them once and for all is when we are young, and mentally and physically vigorous. Later on when the fires burn low and we still have them with us they will be hard to push aside.

"To thine own self be true," says the great Shakespeare and how can we be true to our own

selves if we train with inferiors? We are known
by our companionships. We will be rated according to association—good or bad. The two
will not mix for long and we will be one sort of
a fellow or the other. We can't be both.

There was a time, long years ago, in the days
of our grandfathers, when men went to the "bow-
wows" and, later on, "came back" as it were, by
making a partial success in life—measured
largely by the money they succeeded in accumu-
lating. That was before the "check-up" system
was invented. Today things are different.
Questions are asked—"Where were you last?"—
"Why did you leave there?"—"Have you creden-
tials?"—and when we shake our weary head and
walk away, we fondly wish we had "taken stock"
back there when the "taking" was good.

"To thine own self be true; and it must follow
    as the night the day, thou canst not then be
    false to any man."

When we can analyze ourselves and find that
we are living up to the quoted lines above we may

safely lift the limit from our aspirations. Right
here it is well to say that success is not to be com-
puted in dollars and cents, nor that the will to
achieve a successful life is to be predicated upon
the mere accumulation of wealth. First of all,
good health and good minds—then we may laugh
loud and long—we're safe on "first."

So, with these two weapons we may dig down
into our aspirations, and, keeping in view that our
policy is that of honesty to ourselves and toward
our fellow man, all we need to do is to go about
the program of life cheerfully and stout of heart
—*for now we are in a state of preparedness.*

We are at the point where vision starts. Along
with this vision must come the courage of convictions in order that we may feel that our ideas
are important, and because we have such
thoughts, *we shall surely succeed.* It has often
been noticed that when we have had a large con-
ception and have with force, character, and
strength of will carried it into effect, immediately
thereafter a host of people have been able to say:
"I thought of that myself!" Most of us have

had the same experience after reading of a great discovery that we had thrown overboard because it must not have been "worth while" or someone else would already have thought of it.

The man who puts life into an idea is acclaimed a genius, because he does *the right thing at the right time.* Therein lies the difference between the *genius* and a *commonplace* man.

We all have ambitions, but only the few achieve. A man thinks of a good thing and says: "Now if I only had the money I'd put that through." The word "if" was a dent in his courage. With character fully established, his plan well thought out, he had only to go to those in command of capital and it would have been forthcoming. He had something that capital would cheerfully get behind if he had the courage to back up his claims. To fail was nothing less than moral cowardice. *The will to do* had not been efficient. There was a flaw in the character, after all.

Going back, therefore, to the prescription, we

find that a *sound body*, a *good mind*, an *honest purpose*, and a *lack of fear* are the essential elements of success. So, when we have conceived something for the good of the world and have allowed it to go by default we have dropped the monkey-wrench into the machinery of our preparedness. We must look about us for a reason. Have we fallen by the wayside of carelessness? Have we allowed ourselves to be discouraged by cowardly "ifs"? *Did we lack the sand?* Exactly so; we didn't have the courage of our convictions.

Life is the one great experience, and those who fail to win, if sound of body, can safely lay the blame to their lack of mental equipment. What does it matter if disappointments follow one after the other if we can *laugh and try again?* Failures must come to all of us in some degree, but we may rise from our failures and win back our losses if we are only shrewd enough to realize that good health, sound mind, and a cheerful spirit are necessary adjuncts. As Tennyson says:

"I held it truth, with him who sings
    To one clear harp in divers tones,
    That men may rise on stepping-stones
Of their dead selves to higher things."

All truly great men have been healthy—otherwise they would have fallen short of the mark. Prisons are filled with nervous, diseased creatures. There is no doubt but that most of these who, through ignorance, sifted through to the bottomless pits could have saved themselves had they realized the truth and "taken stock" of themselves, *in time*—of course, allowing for those, who are victims of circumstantial evidence,

The prime necessity of life is health. With this, for mankind, nothing is impossible. But if we do not make use of this good health it will waste itself away and never come back. It often disappears entirely for lack of interest on the part of its thoughtless owner. A little energy would have saved the day. *A little "pep"—and we laugh and live.* Laughter clings to good health as naturally as the needle clings to the magnet.

Over the Hedge and on His Way

It is the outward expression of an unburdened soul. It bubbles forth as a fountain, always refreshing, always wholesome and sweet.

In taking stock of ourselves we should not forget that fear plays a large part in the drama of failure. That is the first thing to be dropped. Fear is a mental deficiency susceptible of correction, if taken in hand before it gains an ascendency over us. Fear comes with the thought of failure. Everything we think about should have the possibility of success in it if we are going to build up courage. We should get into the habit of reading *inspirational books,* looking at *inspirational pictures,* hearing *inspirational music,* associating with *inspirational friends* and above all, we should cultivate the habit of mind of thinking clean, and of doing, wholesome things.

"Guard thyself!" That is the slogan. Let us "take stock" often and see where we stand. We will not be afraid of the weak points. We will *get after them* and get hold of ourselves at the same time. Some book might give us help—a fine play, or some form of athletics will start us to thinking. Self-analysis teaches us to see ourselves in a true light without embellishments or undue optimism. We can gauge our chances in no better way. If we grope in the darkness we haven't much of a chance. "Taking stock" throws a searchlight on the dark spots and points the way out of the danger zone.

CHAPTER III

ADVANTAGES OF AN EARLY START

It is the young man who has the best chance of winning. Then why shouldn't youthfulness be made a permanent asset? We have recovered from the idea of putting a man into a sanatorium just because a few grey hairs show themselves in his head. We should not ask him how old he is . . . we should ask: *"What can he do?"* The young man may have the advantage of years but the older one has the advantage of experience and knowledge. Now if this older man could carry along with him that spirit of youth which actuated his earlier activities he would be prepared against incapacity. Our fate hangs on how we conduct ourselves in youth. The world has great need of the sober, thoughtful men *above the fifty line.* By right of experience and knowledge they should become our leaders in the shaping of our policies. It is all a matter of how a man comes through, mentally, physically and spiritually. Age should not count against him.

The first thought is to keep healthy. In fact, we cannot harp on this too much. The second requirement is confidence in ourselves, without which our career is short lived.

Already we perceive that one must keep track of his *inner self*. This breeds confidence. The very fact that one stops to probe into that hidden land of thought shows that he is keeping tab on himself with a sharp eye. That's the stuff! *We mustn't fool ourselves*. The majority of failures come as a result of not being able to trust one's self. The moment we doubt, or acknowledge that we cannot conquer a weakness, then we begin to go down hill. It is a subtle process. We hardly realize it at the time but as the days go by, the years roll on, the final day of reckoning draws near and relentlessly we are swept along as driftwood toward the lonely beaches of obscurity. And all because *we lacked self-confidence!* We did not realize it until it was too late. We were too busy with self-indulgence to struggle for success.

Most of our troubles in later life started with *failure to take hold of ourselves* when we were young. It may be that we put off making our choice of something to do. If we had been companionable to ourselves we might have thought out the proper course while taking long walks in pursuit of physical development. That would have been a *fine* time in which to fight out the whole problem—the time when optimism and *the will to do* are as natural as the laughter of a child, or the song of a bird. That was the time when the world appeared roseate and beautiful, when success lay just beyond the turn of the road, when failure seemed something illusory and improbable. Then was the time to jump in with both feet and *a big hearty laugh* to solve the problem of what to do and how to go about it. It is surprising how readily the world follows the individual with confidence. It is willing to believe in him, to furnish funds, to assist in any way within its power. And that is where the man *with a smile* is sure to win—for the man who smiles has confidence in himself.

So long as we carry along with us our atmosphere of hearty good will and enthusiasm we know no defeat. The man who is gloomy, taciturn and lives in a world of doubt seldom achieves more than a bare living. There have been a few who have groaned their way through to a competence but in proportion to that overwhelming number of souls who carry cheer through life they are as nothing—mere drops in the bucket. If the truth were told their success came probably through mere chance and nothing else. Such people are not the ones for us to endeavor to follow. *We cannot afford to allow our visions to sour.*

Beginning early takes away timidity and builds for success while we are young enough to enjoy the benefits. Although it is never too late to start a cheerful life we don't have to kill ourselves in the attempt. There is no necessity for throwing all caution to the winds, but we should press our advantages. With *self-analysis* comes a certain poise, a certain dignity and kindliness that tempers every move with precision.

Once we get the proper start we have only to take stock now and then in order to keep our machinery in a fine state of repair. If we have chosen wisely we love our work and stick to it closely—not forgetting the home duties and our share in its success. Right here we run up against the danger signal if our business success wins us away from the hearthstone. *Love of home* is a quality of the workers of the earth. "What doth it profit a man to win the whole world if he *loseth* his own soul?"

To sum up the case—once we have made up our minds to win and how we are going to do it, the next step is to act. *Health is synonymous with action*. The healthy man does things, the unhealthy man hesitates. And when we get ready to act we will act with the air of a conqueror. We must supply from our own store our atmosphere of confidence in order to win confidence. The successful man is the one who *knows he is right* and makes us realize it.

It is always worth while to study the successes among our acquaintances. Are they gloomy, morose and irritable? If they were to that extent they would not be successful. On the contrary, they are robust, confident individuals who have taken advantage of every rightful opportunity and possessed *the power to smile* when all about them were in the dumps. When everyone else thought that there wasn't a chance to win these fellows stepped in and took charge.

When we interview the failures we find that all of them give one excuse: *"I didn't have the confidence."* They may not say it in exactly these words but the meaning is plain. They ran through the whole gamut of *self-distrust* which is the natural result of not having started early in the study of self—the serious realization of their own capabilities.

This makes it easy to understand their plight. If we know ourselves we are strengthened that much, because we can bolster up our weaknesses. We will know enough to combat timidity. We can then know what we are capable of, and thus

Preparing to Pair With the Prickly Pear

become conscious of our innate powers that only need to be called into action in order to become useful. We cannot imagine for an instant a great violinist going out on the concert platform in ignorance of the condition of his instrument. And yet failures go out on the stage of life knowing nothing of their strengths and weaknesses —*and still expect to win!*

If we are to become successes we must *keep success in mind*—banish all thought of losing. Success is just as natural as anything else. It is only a matter of the mind anyhow. We are all successes *as long as we continue to think so.* Self-depreciation is a disease. Once it gets a hold on us—good-bye!

And that is why it is wise to begin early—to take hold of affairs while we are young. Superiority over our fellow man comes from a superiority of mind and body. A healthy mind breeds a healthy body. The most superficial study will convince us of this fact.

Appearance counts for much in this world. We judge largely by appearances. We haven't time to know everyone we meet intimately and as a result must base our opinions upon *first impressions*. The fellow who comes in an office with his head hanging down between his shoulders and a frown upon his face doesn't get far with us. We find ourselves looking over his sagging shoulders toward the individual behind him who comes in with a swinging step and the confidence born of health and good spirits.

Self-confidence in youth makes for self-confidence in after years. This is far from meaning that one can be brazen and inclined towards freshness and get away with it. It merely means the marshalling of one's forces, *the command of one's self* and the ability to make others recognize that we are on the map because we belong there. And one of the quickest ways to accomplish this is to have a smile tucked away for instant use. Again, this does not mean that we are to carry round a ready-to-wear grin which we wear only as we are ushered into the presence of another. *A real smile, or a hearty laugh, is not to be counterfeited.* We easily know the genuine from the spurious. A real laugh springs naturally out of a pure, unadulterated confidence and a good physical condition. What triumphs, what splendid battles, have been won through the ability to laugh at the right moment.

Whenever we find that we are losing our ability to smile let's have no false notions. We are neglecting our physical well being. Let us then and there drop the sombre thoughts and get out into the open air. Run down the street and if possible out into the country. If we see a tree and have the inclination to climb it—well, then, climb it. If we are sensitive about what our neighbors might say—too bad! But we can romp with easy grace. If we but knew how gladly our neighbors would emulate our gymnastics if they knew the value of them the laugh would be on us for dreading their opinion. One thing we do know—*they will envy us our good health and spirits.*

CHAPTER IV

PROFITING BY EXPERIENCE

Experience comes by contact. There is no way we can have experiences without passing directly through them. If we are up and doing they come thick and fast into our lives, some of them weighted down by the peculiar twists and turns of circumstances, others simple, easily understood, and still others complicated to the point of not being understood at all.

People are divided into two classes—*those who profit by experience and those who do not.* The unfortunate part of it all is that the latter class is by far the larger of the two.

The man of vigorous purpose, fine constitution, and the full knowledge of self, sees through an experience as clearly as through a window. The glass may be foggy, but he knows what lies beyond. Self-reliant and strong he seeks knowledge through experience, while the weak man, the unhealthy-minded, the inefficient, stands aside and gives him the right of way. In later years, however, they bitterly complain that they were not given the same chance to succeed.

The man of experience having long since passed through the stages of indecision has, through careful self-analysis learned to bridge difficulties that would make others tremble with fear. He knows that every lane has a turning. He may not see it at the moment. He may not know where it is. *But that doesn't worry him.* He picks up his bundle and trudges ahead, confident that victory awaits him somewhere along the line.

The fact that he believes in himself, sets him apart from ordinary mankind. Many great men have been at loss to understand why they attained success. It is well nigh impossible for them to outline the causes that led them to the top rungs of the ladder. The reason is that *their lack of fear* of experiences was an unconscious one, rather than a conscious one. However, they are willing to admit that acting on the principle of profiting by experience *loaned them initiative* with which to proceed. They soon came to know opportunity at sight and had only to look around to find it.

The young man standing on the threshold of life is, from lack of experience, puzzled over the future. He looks above him and sees the towering successes. He reads in the papers of the massive characters who have risen from the bottom to the top. Naturally he would like to meet one of these giants of success and hear what he has to say. The interview is quite needless. *"Get busy and profit by experience,"* is about all the advice one man can give to another. There is no way to profit by experience until we have had experience so there is nothing to do but get busy and experience will come as fast as we can absorb it. Our duty is to strive for success and not expect to attain it except by successive steps. A wholesale consignment would be our undoing. Quick successes through luck or good fortune have not the lasting value of those won by virtue of knowing how—of accomplishing what we started out to do.

Faith in one's self does not come from the outside—it must spring up naturally *from within.* A healthy body and a sane mind are the best foundations for this. The young man who begins his career with these facts in mind is given a running start over his competitors. Poverty and failure are the result of *an ignorance of the value of experience.* Worry, anxiety, fear of not doing the right thing, lack of insight into character . . . these, too, are the result of a lack of experience.

Good health is necessary to experience, but a majority neglect to take care of it. If we are to profit by what we learn we *must have the vim* with which to push forward. We must have every ounce of vitality we possess at command— ready for use. This we conserve for the *big emergency* which we know is coming. New experiences are pushing us forward and previous experiences are helping to move the load. Experience tells us what to do at this point and that

—and at last puts its shoulder to the wheel and *"over she goes!"*

Every mind is in possession of an enormous amount of dormant power and only experience can release it into proper action. We often hear a fond mother say that her son is full to bursting with the *old nick,* which means that the youngster is overflowing with *pent-up energy.* With experience he could find good use for it—but without it this surplus may turn out to be a dangerous possession. Young men of this type should be guarded most carefully and advised to "get busy" *early in life* at something worth while. Many a bright fellow brimming with excess power has gone as a lamb to the slaughter into the maelstrom of vice because of being held back from *legitimate occupation.* He just had to blow off steam so he did it in a gin mill rather than a rolling mill.

This dynamo called the mind can be trained to do anything. Not only can it be guided at the start but it can be guided by all that follows. It can be used for building additional dynamos to be called into action in times of need. This statement may seem at first far-fetched. If we think so it is proof that we have not *profited by our experiences* and should get down to "stock taking" before it is too late.

The practical man, after all, is only *one who takes advantage of opportunities*. He could double and triple his power if he only realized how superficial the average setback really is. The young man has just as much chance of being considered practical as the so-called older one, always provided that he has a store of experiences to profit by. The first *big experience* of life usually makes or breaks us. For this experience we need to be prepared. We must have a *strong heart* that we may bear defeat nobly from this is not to be our last kick—our last breath—*not by a jugful!*

We are going to start all over again after our setback and we are not going to wait any longer than it takes to bury the dead. This will be done decently and in good order—our training will admit of no indecorum. If the smash was a bad one we will assume the liability, nevertheless, and get back on the job. We are out to win and *eventually we will win.*

And that is what we mean by taking profit from experience. *The powers that break down are also the powers that build up.* The electrician who handles the motor could just as well end his own existence by that mysterious current as he could make use of it for the good of humanity. He spends years of conscientious study and masters the knowledge of it so that its uses are as simple as his A B C's. There is no doubt in the world but that he had to learn by experience. He had to go into the shop and *climb up from the bottom.* There was no other way by which he could come to know how to turn a deadly force into a well-trained necessity.

Yet the average man goes into life with as little knowledge of its forces as the baby who puts its foot upon the third rail. That fact keeps the thoughtless man down until experience comes to the rescue. When it does come, *if he has the sand, the common sense, the will to do,* there is naught to hold him away from his goal.

CHAPTER V

ENERGY, SUCCESS AND LAUGHTER

There are many essentials to success, but there is one that is of such importance that without it all the others become as naught. The man who wins success is invariably impelled to do the great work allotted him by *something within* that tells him *he can.* He may not know exactly what it is, but he knows he possesses it and is able to *act on that faith,* accomplishing things which seem utterly impossible to other people. This *inner determination,* once firmly implanted in one's nature, cannot be destroyed or conquered. And this element is *energy*—energy of mind, which rules the body. But where does this come from? How do the great minds generate this glorious means of self-propulsion? The answer is that *in a healthy body it is inherent* from birth, and proper care of the body therefore accentuates within their minds the will to do.

If the preceding chapters have been carefully read we may readily believe that the successful youth must start with a wholesome, generous viewpoint, a good constitution, and a clean mind. We have had an inkling by this time of what one must do to achieve success in a world where competition is keen. We are beginning to realize that these matters are of vital importance and that we are face to face with a problem.

Energy is the natural outpouring of a healthy body. It must be directed, it must be controlled, the same as any other living force. Not only is it a positive necessity to the winner, but it must grow and become *a natural quality*. It does not stand after years of abuse. It does not spring up in the night after a long season of neglect and ill-health. All of us possess it in varying ways. That fact ought to convince us that we can get hold of ourselves and build up that which nature has given us, rather than allow it to die away. We all have a certain amount of energy . . .

why shouldn't we all be successes? We might to a certain extent, but that doesn't mean that we shall all get rich in the money sense of the world.

When we say: "Why shouldn't we all be successes?" we do not mean that everybody in the world must be greedy for money, nor for power and position. It does not mean that we should be selfish and eager to take everything away from the other fellow. On the contrary, it means that, with energy, we shall be successful *according to our brain tendency.*

Going back to our second chapter we find the phrase "taking stock" of ourselves. Done rightly that alone will inspire success. Now if we are a little farther along on the way towards sane living and the *ability to laugh* and we know that after this struggle is over the battle is won we must use the powers that self-analysis gives us—*to fight*. The mere recognition of them is power and we must not let them go to waste.

Energy is like steam—it cannot be generated under the boiling point. In other words, *half-heartedness* never produced it nor made it a practical working tool. We must be energetic in order to augment energy. We must have confidence along with it . . . the more the merrier. The greater the confidence in ourselves the greater the energy which brought it about. Some minds naturally feel confident. These are the lucky ones, the slender few who have grasped life's meaning at the start by *"taking stock"* before they were threatened with defeat. Success comes to them as easily as rolling off the proverbial log. They come sweeping along, conquering, sure of themselves, confident, aspiring, true to their inner selves, ready for work, unafraid of experiences, and *sure of a smile when the clouds are darkest.*

This does not mean that these successes have exceptional ability. If that were the case we would not waste time either in reading or writing about the matter. If we didn't feel that we were potentially able to become successes and possessed the elements of victory in our present make-up not another moment would be spent on the subject. The very simplicity of this use of energy proves to us that it is a quality bubbling forth *in the least of us* and the strongest. It only needs to be put to work and it becomes self-strengthening. *Living in the open air, sleeping out of doors, taking the proper exercise, looking wholesomely upon life, believing in ourselves,* are all parts of the sane existence which leads to success and laughter.

We ought to feel that everything in life possesses elements akin to human feeling. We should not arrogate to ourselves the sole right to rule and reason. And what has this to do with energy? It is only one of the many vistas that open to us when we learn how to laugh and live. And man alive! *If we never learn to laugh we will never learn to live.*

We must not forget that there can be more than one use made of energy. In the same way that electricity might be misused so might energy be placed in the wrong service. We must not waste any time, therefore, in getting this energy of ours worked into *enthusiasm* . . . enthusiasm for our life work, for our fellow man, *for the zest of life.* We must throw ourselves into the battle and carry the standard. We must leap to the front, not waiting for the other fellow to show the way. Spend your enthusiasm freely and be surprised at how it thrives on usage.

Enthusiasm being produced by energy must of a necessity depend largely upon that. Now the point is, how shall we guard and keep fresh this element in ourselves? We know that the body is producing this quality. Like the steam engine we are keeping the fires going by exercise, wholesome thinking and sincerity of purpose. We are the engineers. Our hand is on the throttle. Sharp turns lie ahead but our eyes look forward fearlessly. We glance about us to see that we are in the pink of condition. We know that our mind is functioning properly and that the awakened confidence is already inherent in our natures and stands beside us night and day like the officer upon the bridge of the ship. *Indeed we are on our way!*

Out of energy and enthusiasm comes something else that must not be neglected . . . in fact

A Little Spin Among the Saplings

it must be cultivated and guarded from the very beginning . . . *laughter*. The mere possession of energy and enthusiasm makes us feel like laughing. We want to leap and jump and dance and sing. If we feel like that don't let us be afraid to do it. *Get out in the air and run like a school boy. Jump ditches, vault fences, swing the arms!* Never fail to get next to nature when responsive to the call. Indeed we may woo this call from within ourselves until it comes to be second nature. And when we rise in the morning let us be determined that we will start the day with a hearty laugh anyhow. Laugh because you are alive, laugh with everything. *Let yourself go*. That is the secret—the ability to let one's self go!

If we follow this religiously we will be surprised how successful the day will be. Everything gives way before it.

CHAPTER VI

BUILDING UP A PERSONALITY

More and more personality is coming into its own as man's greatest asset. There was never a day when it was not, but in former years this essential quality was not listed under the name . . . *personality*. Had we lived in the days of our fathers' youth we would have heard about "remarkable men," "men of big caliber," "large character," "splendid presence," and the like. But it remained for our day and generation to discover the real word—*personality*—meaning the *most perfect combination possible of man's highest attributes*. At least that would be the definition in its fullest sense.

Of course everyone has a certain personality and, no matter in what degree, its possession is valuable. Personality is an acorn, so to speak,

which may be cultivated into a sturdy oak.   Personality is one's *inner self outwardly expressed.*
It represents the conquest of our weaknesses and
naturally impresses our strength of character
upon others.

With personality our foundation is firm.   On
this pedestal we may stand squarely and face
life with equanimity.   For such there is no end
to achievement while good health and youthful
spirit remain.

It is impossible to come into the presence of
a personality without becoming immediately
aware of it.   It is reflected by people of *small
stature . . . poor physiques . . . homely visages,*
as well as men of the highest physical development.   The great Napoleon was just above five
feet while Lincoln towered over the six-foot line.
Men of personality are the last to say die.   Their
store of *combativeness* carries them beyond their
real span of existence either in years or achievement.   Thus, the mind shows its mastery over
matter.   Alexander Pope was still writing while
propped upon the pillows of his death bed.   Mark

Twain joked with friends when he knew his hour was at hand.

Personality is magnetic. It can charm the friend or put fear into the heart of the enemy. Joan of Arc, a frail woman, won battles at the head of her troops. History is filled with incidents where men of personality have turned defeat into victory by leading their soldiers back into the fray.

Wholesome personality is the fulfillment of self-development—physically, mentally and spiritually. But all personality is not wholesome for it often shows in the face of the man *who is a rogue at heart.* Therefore, all personality is not for the good of the world. It is only of the wholesome kind that we speak. To such as possess it the goal is divine. Personality could never be perfected without living a *life of preparedness* backed up by our most earnest and honest convictions. Personality is made up of many qualities and differs in man only as man is different from his brother man. Perfect personality requires constant care in its development and constant guard for its safety. It cannot be purchased in the open market. It must be built upon piece by piece and everything we are becomes a part of it.

Personality would be indeed imperfect if it did not give us *full poise*. If we neglect our physical poise we pull down our mental poise, likewise our spiritual poise. That is why personality must be kept constantly protected against encroachment; but this can be so fixed by purpose, plan, and power of will that it becomes automatically safeguarded. Once in possession we have only to make it part of our natural selves and *wear it unconsciously* to the last breath of life.

Then the question is, why should we allow ourselves to be satisfied with an imperfect personality? It only reflects back upon ourselves. Haven't we often heard a man say: *"He is all right but . . . !"* Perhaps the personality in question was untidy, or that his walk was that of a laggard, or that he affected an egotistical air of superiority—whatever the impairment it should have been done away with.

A man of personality should never be haunted with worry from the sneers of his inferiors because of their own laxity. Some men perfect their manner of speech to a degree which takes it above that of their weaker fellows, others develop fine qualities which are viewed by ordinary individuals as affectations but which are in reality the result of *innate refinement.*

The man of no refinement has indeed an up-hill fight but with persistence and ambition to succeed he can win. Lincoln, the rail splitter, is the most shining example of *the power to will victory.* For him to have fallen by the wayside would have caused no comment for it would have been expected in those early days of struggle, but to those who have the benefit of inherited tendencies toward personality, to fail in its development is in the nature of a crime.

Personality does not mean over-refinement. *Sturdy qualities* are the necessary ones. Over-refinement leads to the softer life and ofttimes to degeneracy. Exalted ego is an indication of degeneracy and may have been inherited. Of those things we inherit that are good we must hold, and everlastingly must we watch those which are bad. It is never wise to wander far away from basic principles into preachment. What we need is guidance along the road to the goal of personality. First of all we need *health* and second, *the will to do*. Next, we must use these weapons in the right direction, for personality is at its zenith when backed up by *strong physique and brain power*.

From previous chapters we have learned that success of any kind is predicated upon keeping ourselves in trim, and in good humor. Keeping in trim is no trick at all. We can make it a part of every physical action and as keeping in trim means perfection of body and soundness of mind we should never neglect to utilize any effort that will help us toward bodily efficiency. *There is exercise in stooping over to pick up a pin if we will go about it the right way. We can correct an ill-formed body by adopting and maintaining a certain carriage. We may hold our chin in such a way as to provide against stooped shoulders.*

We have opportunities both morning and evening to indulge in various forms of light, systematic exercises which will push forward the day's work with zest and vim.

Poise has everything to do with personality, therefore the physical structure must come in for its share of proper attention. No man of refined personality would walk the streets with a soiled face or uncombed hair. Such things do not give poise. They are the evidences of a laggard spirit. The more we exercise the more energetic we become, the surer we are of ourselves, the farther we get in the development of our personality.

White Studio

Over the Hills and Far Away—Father and Son

CHAPTER VII

HONESTY, THE CHARACTER BUILDER

Just as the straight line is the shortest distance between two points so is honesty the only proper attitude of one person toward another. Without it there is no understanding possible. It must always remain supreme as a quality without which character becomes a sham, a superficial thing that has no basis in fact. *The ability to look the other fellow in the eye* is as necessary to character as the foundation is to a house. It comes out of that *"great within"* which we are now exploring. It arises from the courageous facing of our weaknesses and becomes a part of the man *who knows himself and laughs with life,* at the mere joy of living, doing, accomplishing . . . winning against all odds.

Honesty accompanies a proper self-esteem and its cultivation should become a part of our earliest education. It doesn't grow anywhere except within ourselves and will never be handed to us on a silver platter. If we fail to find it when we are young it will have small chance of obtaining a grip on us later. *It is the one quality with which to crown our highest attributes.* It is final proof that we are capable of just thought and square dealing, and is proof positive that we are part and parcel of the wholesome spirit which rules the universe. Its possession is greater than riches for its dividend is happiness and contentment and we cannot go wrong if we so live that we can look any man in the eye and *tell him the truth.*

To live in the full sense means to be alert. Whatever high moral plane we shall achieve must be held against all temptation. There is no compromise. *Self-deceit* is nothing less than *self-stultification.* We only fool ourselves and soon find ourselves slipping down hill. It will be hard climbing getting back. And what of the wear and tear on our ambitions meanwhile!

Honesty does not grow naturally out of a

dull, uninspired life. It goes with the energetic, the forceful. The dull soul who is content to plod along year after year in the same rut may be honest, and this one redeeming feature may be of such inestimable value to him that it sweetens and softens his entire days. It will bring him friends . . . true-blue friends, who will excuse all other shortcomings *because of his honesty*. It gives him the unadulterated trust of his employer and it arouses a certain admiration among his narrow circle of acquaintances. If this is true with the dullard, the weakling, then what must it mean *when possessed by the great?* We know, for instance, how the nation instinctively turned to General Washington when it came to choosing their President after the Revolutionary War. He may have been gifted, he may have been one of the world's greatest captains, but the one quality which endeared him to his countrymen was a tremendous moral superiority. *"He never told a lie"* rang around the world. Summed up, his virtues amounted to those five words. Some statesmen may have been more astute but Washington was honest—*"he never told a lie."* The people knew they could trust this man so they elected him to fill the highest place within their gift.

Honesty with ourselves is the first thing to remember. Unless we are, it will be impossible for us to enter into that spiritual contentment enjoyed by those who *are* honest with themselves. If we are untrue to ourselves how can we be true to others? The framework of a man's moral being must be that of honesty. It must become his very nature and become automatic in its processes. It belongs to the healthy, those who keep themselves well through *vigorous exercise and temperate living.* It is not a quality set aside for the lucky few. Every man, woman and child possesses it in some degree and only its constant neglect trims it to a minimum. It is one of those fundamentals of life, one of those powerful and moving forces that rule society. *We are either honest or we are not.* We cannot be *nearly honest* and get away with it.

When one stops to consider honesty, even for a

moment, its full importance is realized. For example, imagine having a dishonest friend. Could we go to him with the secrets of our heart? Could we trust him? Would we trust anyone who might turn traitor? Again: suppose we were untrue to ourselves, and the fact became known. Could we blame others if they passed us up as a companion? Never in a thousand years. *We must sleep in the beds we prepare for ourselves.*

Men have grown accustomed through the years to certain standards. These are now the moral laws which control and guide the destinies of entire races, whole generations. There must have been a good reason for these laws or they could never have come into being. Society does not adopt many unnecessary rules, but among the vital laws *honesty stands out in bold relief*. It has become deeply imbedded in the minds of mankind that everyone must be true to himself. It is taken for granted that those who are not would naturally be *false to everybody*.

The reason for this lies in the fact that society

will not proceed with any course of action without being able to trust its members. The general in charge of an army would have a hard time of it if he were unable to place faith in the subordinate to whom he gave instructions that might lead to a crisis in the battle. Society would dash itself upon the rocks were it not conscious that certain people are courageously honest, *and in these it finds its leaders.*

To rise in life means that our fellow man believes in us and wishes us to do so. Without his co-operation it would be futile to arouse our own ambitions. We could not hope to win a victory all alone and against the great majority who believe in certain standards and conditions. We might fool ourselves into thinking that because of some stroke of fortune we had established an immunity for ourselves. But some day *our consciences* would tell us how feebly we had succeeded.

There is only one method, only one way . . . rise through honesty and an optimistic belief in self. And let us not plume ourselves because of our virtue. *Personal honesty is our due to ourselves and our fellow man.*

One of the distinctive elements in the honest man's make-up is that of laughter. The ones who live up to their ideals, do not feel that life is such a dark place, after all. It may mean hard work, little play and often delayed rewards but the fact that there is a world, and that it is filled with other honest souls is reward enough to give us courage to laugh as we go along. *We can always afford to laugh—when we're honest.*

The man who is innately honest has no reason to fear the snares of fortune. He knows that he can win the trust of men; he knows that he already has it. He has no dread of looking into the other fellow's eye. He knows where he stands in life. He has won that which he has through struggle, and he does not intend to lose it. He does not intend to fail. *He cannot fail—he cannot lose.* No matter how things might go at this moment or that the next will find him on the rising tide of new opportunities—new chances. His reputation travels before him like

the advance agent.   His coming is heralded and
he is welcomed into any community.

It isn't as though there were only a few honest
men.   This welcome, this "glad hand," is always
extended by society to the honest man as a token
of approval.   The world's work is a tremendous
matter.   There is always room for another worker
to handle some part of it.   And only the true, the
sincere, are capable of doing this in the proper
way.   The leaders of society in the broader sense
are those *who win the faith of the average man*.
We look up to Lincoln because we know that he
was the one man in a million to accomplish the
greatest task ever set before a human being.   We
realize that he was honest—*honest in the huge
sense* so necessary to the accomplishment of big
ideals.   And we know that in order to win some
part of that great trust we must obey the standards of honesty and decency that lie below the
surface and only need to be called to life and
action in order to be used.

And laughter will arouse that sense as quickly
as anything else.   The man who is capable of

A Scene from "His Picture in the Papers"

laughing heartily is not apt to be the one who carries some *conscience-stricken thought around with him*. It is the easiest thing in the world to detect an untrue laugh. The real laugh springs out of the depths of being and comes with a ringing sense of security and *faith in one's self*. It goes with the workman in the early morning when he swings along the road to the factory. It accompanies the soldier into battle. It arouses the clerk from lethargy. It brightens the sick room. It raises us all to unexplored heights, and as evidence of our state of mind it can only mean one thing—honesty and sincerity. No character can exist without this outward exhibition of an inward honesty. *The mere cultivation of laughter would eventually lead to honesty*. The fact that you are laughing, enjoying life, awakens you to a spirit of security and a feeling of the joy of living. Gloomy men are the ones whose tendency is toward crime and trouble. Laughing men are the ones who stir the world with new desires and make life worth living. Therefore we say—*laugh and live!*

CHAPTER VIII

CLEANLINESS OF BODY AND MIND

If we interview many of life's failures we will find that the overwhelming majority went down because of their neglect to get out of an environment that was not stimulating and because their ambitions had grown rusty and inefficient to cope with depressing circumstances. The prisons and other institutions are filled with people who did not make any attempt to get away from the vicious surroundings in which they lived. They were like tadpoles that had never grown to frogs . . . they just kept swimming around in their muddy puddles and, not having grown legs with which they could leap out onto the banks and away to other climes, they continued to swim in monotonous circles until they died. In other words, the failure is a man who dwells in muddy atmosphere all his days, who is content to remain a tadpole and who never attempts to take advantage of any opportunity. He becomes unclean, so to speak. And that is what we mean by this chapter heading *"Cleanliness of Body and Mind."* It was not intended to point out the proper way to keep our faces and hands clean, or as a sermon, but rather to show ourselves that *the clean body begets the clean mind,* the two together constituting compelling tendencies toward *the clean spirit.* A move in the direction of these takes us out of the rut of life.

No matter what cause we dig up with which to explain our success in life we cannot neglect this most important one—*the careful selection of our acquaintances.* And this doesn't mean that one must be a snob. Far from it. It only means that the successful man, the man who wishes to rise in life, should not spend his days in the company of *illiterate companions* who do not possess *ambition of heart or the will to do the work of the world.* It means that life is too short to hang around the loafing places with the driftwood of humanity listening to their stories

of failure and drinking in with liquor some of
their bitterness against those who have toiled and
won the fruits of their toil. It means that we
will not go out of our way to seek the friendship of men and women who are simply endeav-
oring to gain happiness in life without paying
for it. It means that we will do all in our power
to win friends who *aspire nobly* and by so doing
inspire those with whom they come in contact.
Such men are naturally clean of mind and body.

We must remember always to live in a world
of clear thought that will *stimulate our ambitions*.
Dwelling in the dark corners of life and traveling
with the débris of humanity will not arouse us
to action and give us that swinging vigor of heart
and mind so necessary to the accomplishment of
great things. While we will ever lend the helping hand to those who need it we will naturally
associate with those who have vim and courage.
We will not be *dragged down by our associates*.
Until we meet the right kind we will hold aloof,
and we will not be morose and gloomy because
it happens that at this moment our acquaintance-

ship does not include these successes. When we have succeeded in doing something big they will come to us and *if we think big things we are likely to do them*. It is all a matter of the will to do.

"Nothing succeeds like success," said some very wise man and if there ever was a phrase that rang with truth this does. It means that the *thought of success,* the courage that *comes with success,* leads to *more and more success.* It means that the thinker of these thoughts is living in a clean, wholesome atmosphere along with those who are determined and in earnest. It means that they have caught the fervor of true life . . . a healthy, contagious fervor which permeates the blood swiftly once it gets a hold, and like electricity it vivifies and stirs the spirit with renewed energy *day after day, year after year.* Once it wins us it will stick with us. The success of those about us will shake our lethargic limbs and stimulate us to a desire to do as they do. We will be in a world of clean thought and action and our lives will mirror their lives, our thoughts will be filled with wholesome things and with good health. We will win in spite of all obstacles.

Cleanliness is *the morale of the body and the mind*. The man who is careful of his linen and who does not neglect his morning plunge is not apt to be gloomy and morose. We notice him in the car or on the street in the morning. He comes striding along, fresh and full of *the zest of living*. His mind is clear and unclouded. His eyes are full of that vigorous light of conscientious desire to win and do so honestly. He has none of the hypocritical elements in his nature strong enough to rule him. There may be and probably are many weaknesses in his character. His very strength consists in his ability to *crush them and make them his slaves*.

The man who has taken his morning plunge and dressed himself agreeable to comfort and grace, has his battles of the day won in advance. He knows the value of keeping himself in trim. He does it for the sake of *his own* feelings. Our approval of his appearance goes without saying.

If a man thinks well of himself in matters of appearance his general deportment is likely to coincide. Such men never overdo. They are at ease with themselves and thus impart ease to others who come in contact with them. They have, in other words, a distinction of their own and *their distinction is their power*. They know that the highest moral law of nature is that of cleanliness, that filthiness should not be allowed to dominate any man's ethics or physical condition. They rule such things out of their lives.

A vast magnetic force comes out of those friends of ours who are *doing things* and making the world *sit up and take notice*. The mere fact that we live near to them, know them and associate with them is proof-positive that we, too, shall go through life with clean minds and bodies. They would not tolerate us if we were to slip into shoddy ways. Nothing is revealed quicker to our intimates than *the losing of ambition* . . . the slipping into careless habits. We cannot conceal it from them. We fool only those who brush by. The loss of this self-respect has a terrible effect upon the system and every tendency toward success is thereby stunted and weakened. *We have fallen into unclean ways!* It will not be long before we sink to the bottom or else remain among the vast crowd who have neither the courage to fall nor the courage to rise.

Nothing produces failure quicker than filthiness of mind and body. Those who are successful keep away from the very thought of such a condition. They live as much as possible *in the open*. They take morning and evening exercises. They read good books, attend good plays and are continually in touch with the finer developments of thought and art in the world. Their faces are open and full of sunlight. They are determined that life will not beat them in a game that only requires sureness of aim and the ability to take advantage of the thousand and one opportunities that surround them on every side.

Cleanliness stands *paramount* in its importance to *success*. Perhaps no other one thing has so vital a hold upon the individual who succeeds. The general of an army first looks to the *morale* of his troops. He knows that with clean minds and bodies his soldiers are capable of doing big things. The battleship, that efficient and highly-developed instrument of war, is so immaculate that one could eat his meals on its very decks. Its officers are wholesome, athletic fellows; its crew consists of hardy men who live sanely and vigorously and who have plenty to occupy their minds. And if cleanliness is fundamental in their case why not in our own?

When we come to analyze ourselves we find that we are like a great institution of some kind. Here is the brain, the heart, the lungs, the stomach, the nerves and the muscles. Each department acts separately and yet is connected absolutely with all the others. The entire system is under one supreme department . . . *the mind*. Now if this ruling department is kept clean and full of kindly, beautiful thoughts does it not seem natural that the rest will follow its lead being so completely in its power? We realize this and the mere realization is something done towards the accomplishment of an ideal life in a world of cleanliness and beauty.

System is one of the finest tools in existence with which to build one's life into something worth while. The *body* must be run on a system as well as the *mind*. The stomach must not be overloaded with unnecessary food. The lungs must not be filled with impure air. The nerves must not be worn threadbare in riotous and ridiculous living. The muscles must be kept in trim with consistent exercise of the proper sort. We must recognize the wants, the needs of the physical system and see that they are supplied.

Roosevelt, perhaps more than any other living man today, has given vitality to the supreme necessity of *cleanliness of mind and body*. He has, by reason of his great prominence, been able to emphasize these two vital essentials. He called a spade a spade and his message went far. From those who knew the value of his words came nods of approval—*others took heed*. From boyhood he has systematized his life, taking the exercise needed, filling his mind with the learning of the world, winning when others would have failed, profiting by experience allotted to him through fate's kindly offices and association with the *healthy, true men.* What has been the result? He has risen to the very pinnacle of human endeavor . . . *no honors await him.* He has lived consistently and cleanly and he can look any man in the eye and say honestly: *"I have lived as I have believed."*

It is not necessary to become President in order to live sanely, to gain from circumstances the fruits that are ours for the asking and which have fallen into Roosevelt's hands with such profusion. We cannot all become Presidents but we can all *emulate a shining example of mental and bodily morale.*

Just as we plunge into the cold water in the early morning so should we regularly during the day plunge into the society of those whose splendid enthusiasm is helping to make the world a better place to live in. They are the kind who go into the struggle with heads high and with clean hearts. Their eyes see beyond the daily toil of life. They are in touch with the big things and it is up to us to keep step with them. They want us and they will give us the "glad hand." All they want to know is whether our courage is equal to our ambitions and whether our *house of life is kept in good order*. And so we journey along together in all good nature, not forgetting to laugh as we live.

CHAPTER IX

CONSIDERATION FOR OTHERS

Consideration for others is man's noblest attitude toward his fellow man. For every seed of human kindness he plants, *a flower blooms in the garden of his own heart.* In him who gives in such a way there is no hypocritical feeling of charity bestowed. His very act disarms the thought. It is as natural for an honorable man to show consideration to others as it is for him to eat and sleep. Acts of kindness are the *outward manifestations of gentle breeding*—a refinement of character in the highest sense of the word.

What would we do in this world without the helping hand, the friendly word of cheer, the thought that others shared our losses and cheered our victories? If consideration for our feelings

and thoughts did not exist on this earth we would
never know the depths of the love of our
friends. There would be no such thing as an
earthly reward of merit. We know that no
matter what happens to us in the battle of life
there will be someone to cheer us on our way.
We may be strong and thoroughly able to rely
upon ourselves but there comes a time when we
need friendship and sympathy. Society would
crumble into dust without these influences. The
family circle would degenerate into a hollow
mockery if consideration each for the other was
absent. It sweetens and makes wholesome what
otherwise might only be an existence of monotonous toil.

Consideration for others is *the milk of human
kindness*. For what we do for others our recom-
pense is *in the act itself* . . . we should claim no
other reward. Observation brings to view that
they who give in real charity *cloak their acts from
the eyes of all save the recipient*. Givers of this
type rise to the supreme heights of greatness. It
is a part of their wisdom to know what is best

to be done and they go about it as a pleasure as well as a duty.

Consideration for others pays big dividends. It is a virtue that makes for strong friendships and true affections. Those who possess it have a hard time hiding their light under a bushel. In teaching fortitude to others they partake of the same knowledge. In the hours of their own affliction they retain their courage and keep their minds unsoured. They are the *sure-enough "good fellows" of life* and their presence is the signal for instantaneous good cheer. We all know them by their gentle knock at the door. In a thousand ways they impress themselves upon our lives, have entered into our councils, have given us the right advice at the right time—and when the sad day comes along *their strong shoulders are there for us to lean upon.*

Consideration for others is apt to be an inherent quality, but like everything else it can be accentuated or modified according to our own determination. It is a growth that should be inculcated *early in the lives of children*—the earlier the bet-

ter. A child's most impressionable age is said
to be between its fourth and fifth years. Then
is the time to teach it the little niceties of life—
the closing of a door softly—tip-toeing quietly
that mother may not be awakened from her
nap—tidiness—cleanliness—good morals—all of
which are to become vital factors in a life of consideration for others.

A great many of us have the desire to be of
service to others but *timidity* holds us back. Say,
for instance, one might see a person in great distress and because of diffidence withhold the prof-
fered hand—someone we've known who comes to
the point of penury but has *too much pride* to
ask assistance—we pass by fearful that we might
offend. How many times has this happened to
us? Who knows but the best friend we have
at this very moment would give anything in the
world if his pride would let him bridge that distance between us.

Nevertheless the desire to do the right thing
was in itself helpful. The thought of doing
something for someone was a correct impulse and

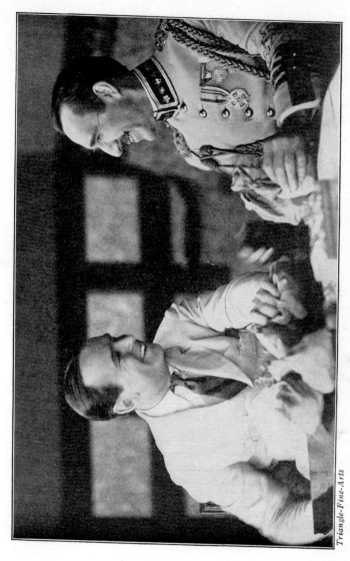

Triangle-Fine-Arts

A Scene from "The Americano"—Matching Wits for Gold

should have been carried into action. Early in life we should have started our foundation for doing things in the cause of others. Putting off the time when we shall begin to obey our higher impulses toward helpfulness to our fellows is but a reaction in our own characters which *dulls determination*. We want to do but we don't. As time goes on we just *don't*—that's all. Our good intentions have gone to pave the bottomless pits containing our unfulfilled heart promptings. We meant well—*but we failed to act*—we didn't have the courage. Our failures spread a gloom before us. *We lost our chances for a happy life!*

The man with the ability to laugh has little diffidence about these matters. Having confidence in himself and being happy and alert he goes to the friend in need with courage and the kind of help that helps. If he doesn't do it directly he finds a way to reach him through mutual friends. He does not go about *parading* his kindness, either. He has gained a sincere and beautiful pleasure out of aiding an old friend and he can go on his way rejoicing that life is worth living when he has lived up to its higher ideals.

Consideration for others does not necessarily involve only the big things. It is the sum and total of numberless acts and thoughts that make for friendships and kindliness. People who are thoughtful surely brighten the world. They are ever ready to do some little thing at the correct moment and after a time we begin to realize how much their presence means to us. We may not notice them the first time, or the third, or the fifth, but after a while we become conscious of their persistence and we esteem them accordingly. Such men are the products of *clean, straightforward lives.* They are never too busy to exchange a pleasant word. They do not flame into anger on a pretext. Their code of existence is well ordered and filled to the brim with lots to do and lots to think about. The old saying: *"If you want anything go to a busy man,"* applies to them in this regard. The busier men are the more time they seem to have for *kindliness.*

Another word for consideration is service. Nothing brings a greater self-reward than a service done in an hour of need, or a favor granted during a day's grind. The generous man who climbs to the top of the ladder helps many others on their way. The more he does for someone else the more he does for *himself.* The stronger he becomes—the greater his influence in his community. Doing things for others may not bring in *bankable dividends* but it does bring in *happiness.* Such actions scorn a higher reward. We have only to try out the plan to learn the truth for ourselves. A good place to begin is *at home.* Then, *the office,* or wherever life leads us. And in doing these things we will laugh as we go along—we will laugh and get the most out of living.

Our little day-by-day kindnesses when added together constitute in time a huge asset on the right side of our ledger of life. We should start the day with something that helps another get through his day . . . even if it isn't any more than a smile and a wave of the hand." And he will remember us for it.

It is said that advice is cheap and for that

reason is given freely. But the proper kind of advice is about as rare as the proverbial hen's tooth. In order to give real advice we must understand the man who asks for it. If what we say to him is to become of value we must see to it that his mind is put in proper shape to receive advice. Be sure that he laughs, or smiles at least, before we seriously take up his case. And when we have done our stunt in the way of advice let's send him away with a fine good humor. A friendly pat on the back as he goes out our doorway may mean a bracer to his determination. *"You'll put it over,"* we shout after him—and thus we have been of real help. He needed sympathy and courage. He needed a cheerful spirit —so came to us and we didn't let him go away until we gave him all these. Bully for us!

Consideration for others does not admit of ostentation and hypocrisy. We never allow our left hand to know what our right hand does in charity, nor do we *boast of our helpful attitude toward our fellow men.* It is well to make a point of this fact—in this world are many *"ne'er-*

do-wells" who fail to profit by advice and thereby become professional in the seeking of favors. Consideration owes them nothing and to withstand their persistent appeals would in time *dull our natural tendencies* toward helping others.

The world helps those who help themselves. We have little admiration for the man who is forever whining. Society has no work for such people as these. When we have exhausted every means of helping such a man we must in self-defense pass him up before he contaminates our sense of justice. *We must keep our visions clear.*

Consideration for others is a prime refinement of character. To be able to use it in our daily lives becomes one of our greatest consolations. Sympathy begets affection and kindly deeds—in a relative sense it binds together the properties which go to make *the soul within us.* Browbeating, scolding, irascibility and the like are microbes which react against the milk of human kindness, to which, if we succumb, leaves us stranded and alone amid a world of friendliness and good fellowship.

CHAPTER X

Big words and pomposity never were designed for the highest types of men. Our great national figures have almost without exception had one quality which was a keynote to their ultimate success—this was their *simplicity*. Next was their *accessibility*. There are numberless big-hearted and big-brained individuals in the world whose duties are so manifold that in order to accomplish what has been placed in their hands they must be saved from interruption, but the truly great individual is never hidden away entirely from his fellow man. He never becomes such a slave to detail that he does not find time to fraternize with ordinary mortals. We do not find him concealed behind impenetrable barriers, guarded and pampered by courtiers like unto a king on his throne—or tucked away in some dark

office. He wants to know *everybody worth while*
and everybody worth while is welcomed by him.
He doesn't affect to know so much that he cannot be told something new. He is not the sort
to refuse to see us at any reasonable time.

We should not confound *greatness,* however,
with *notoriety.* A man who by virtue of large
publicity has compelled public notice isn't necessarily a great man no matter how hard he may
strive to make himself appear so. Especially is
this true of the man who does not make a personal
success corresponding to his advertised fame.
In time he may have the "ear-marks" of notabil-
ity but, as Lincoln said: *"You can't fool all of
the people all of the time."*

It is to be noted with satisfaction that the big
captains of industry keep themselves free from
petty details. "I surrounded myself with clever
men," said Andrew Carnegie in accounting for
his success and by the same token the men who
took over his great affairs and gave them larger
scope and power surrounded themselves with still
other clever men, thus reserving their judgment

and thought *for the higher policies of their institutions.* They keep themselves in readiness for
consultation, and having men of *initiative* and
self-reliance underneath them, they find time to
take in hand other affairs than those of the tremendous businesses they manage. Men of this
type often become prominent in public affairs
and develop into highly important citizens.

The bigger the man, the less he encumbers
himself with matters which can be delegated to
others. His desk is clear of all litter and
minutia—*likewise his mind.* Such men keep
their physiques and mentalities in fine working
order and are not to be goaded into *ill temper.*
A refinement of mind is supremely essential to
the man who desires to climb to the very top of
the ladder. He cannot afford to close his brain
to outside information. He is forced to keep it
open in order to let in continuous currents of
new thought. He doesn't want his visage to
"cream and mantle as a standing pond" as
Shakespeare aptly puts it—therefore the windows
of his thinking department are kept open for

Taking on Local Color

refreshing draughts from the outside. He reasons that always there are new guests, new faces, new things to talk about at the banquet board of life.

And here is the point—if men who carry on the great industries of the world find a way to keep themselves democratic surely men of less importance should be able to do the same? The snob is about as offensive a person as could be described. He is usually a hypocrite or an ignoramus—sometimes both. His pomposity is naturally repellent. We easily become accustomed to dodging such characters. The detriment is theirs—not ours. They are left by the wayside and sooner or later wake up to the fact that they stand alone in the world.

The world loves the man with *an open mind*. This is the usual spirit of the progressive citizen. *He wants to know*—and by reason of his accessibility knowledge is brought to him. No one cares to take up the task of informing the egotist who already knows it all. Such is his inherent cussedness that we would rather let him warp in the oven of his own half-baked knowledge. Life is too short to waste our time in educating him.

"How can I see Mr. So-and-so?" says one man to another.

"Don't try," is the answer. "He's not worth seeing. You can't tell *him* anything."

And this sort of a chap misses the big opportunities just because he chooses to build up a reputation for being exclusive. He digs himself a hole and crawls into it *and pulls the hole in after him.* We can safely imagine him treating the members of his family as though they were servants, and his employees as though they were slaves. He may succeed in small things but in the big game of life we may write him down as a failure.

If we have a big idea we take it to a big man —*the man of vision.* Anything less is to putter around aimlessly. The bigger he is, the more democratic. He will not look for imperfections in our personal make-up when we show him the *new process* we have discovered.

To be democratic is a triumph of the soul—

tending to bring us in close touch with the throbbing heart of humanity. There is no isolation for those of unaffected charm and manner—no barrier in the way of friendship worth having. It is our lack of judgment if we hide ourselves so that we cannot be approached. No matter how high we rise, for the sake of our own brains we must allow *men of ideas* to get to us. We must not allow our minds to become stagnant. If we fail to get into daily contact with other people, we soon grow dull and uninteresting even to ourselves. Great men may have no time to fritter away but they have plenty of leisure for men worth while—*the pushers and the thinkers.*

A democratic spirit does not come to the selfish man. He is absorbed in himself and is quite a hopeless case. He is a natural born faultfinder and grouchy by nature. For him life holds no joy save the one in sight. Taking the big look at the man of this type we can only be sorry for him because of his lack of early training. He started off on the wrong foot and thereafter drifted along. Seldom do we overcome the habits with which we arrive at man's estate. Those who do are entitled to a right hand seat among the chosen.

Being democratic is another phrase for being *human and kind*. It means that we ought to be able to see behind every face and find the truth of that individual's existence. It means that life is largely a matter of how we look at it and being human is one way to get the proper slant at things.

The human mind has *great adaptive power* and can be molded into a thousand ways of thinking. The intelligent man, the man who has taken stock of himself, is able to smile and extend a hearty handclasp whether he feels tip-top or not. He doesn't have to look glum simply because the world hasn't thrown itself at his feet. He has only to persevere and success will come eventually.

We must correct our failings as we go along or we will slip down into the rut and stay there. It is a simple matter to be good natured and full of the zest of life if we poise ourselves right—

keep ourselves democratic. It is this great soul quality which brings us true friends and boosts us into the fulfillment of our ambitions. Then we may truly *laugh and live.*

CHAPTER XI

SELF-EDUCATION BY GOOD READING

The character of a man expresses itself by the books he reads. Every well-informed man since the invention of printing has been a close reader of a few books that stand out from among the many. We read of Lincoln devouring the few books he had, over and over again and studying from cover to cover and word for word the Webster's dictionary of his day. We know that Grant had his favorite volumes from which he drew inspiration and solace. These men made eternal friends of certain great thinkers and drank in their learning with all the fervor of their natures.

"A few good books, digested well, do feed
   The mind."

"Feed the mind!" That's the idea—*but how shall we feed it?* The answer is easy—with some-

thing *worth while*—something that will inform
and inspire. We can cram our minds to the point
of indigestion with useless, frivolous information
just as easily as we may cram our stomachs with
certain foods that tear down rather than build
up. The habit of reading the right sort of books
should begin early in life and continue throughout our days.

Good books are real . . . and as we read we
feel, hear, see and understand in the way the
author did. If what is said appeals to our way
of thinking *a new world* is unfolded to our vision
filled to the brim with things we can think about
and add to our stock of knowledge. While we
are buried in its leaves we may live over the
thoughts that the writer lived. For the time being he becomes as real and vital to us as the dear-
est friend we possess. Gradually, as the time
passes by, he creeps into our affections until our
lives would not be complete without the comradeship of his cherished book.

Books that become our "pals" are not necessarily books of the so-called classical type. Lit-

tle known volumes may prove to have enough thought stored away between their covers to keep us interested all our days. The great books will prove their worth in a short time no matter how poor the binding, how bad the type or how cheap the paper. These things are after all only the outward manifestations and though we like to see our friends dressed well yet we know that the clothes do not make character unless there is character there in the first place. And so it is with books. These little ungainly volumes which we purchase on the stands may be the classics of tomorrow . . . who knows?

We select our library carefully. No matter if we live in a tiny hall bedroom on the top floor of a boarding house we have a shelf somewhere with a few good books on it. Emerson's "Essays" can be had in one volume and are well worth having. No other American writer has been so inspiring, so invigorating as this thinker of Concord. One cannot read his essays without having a desire to *get up and do*. It is like a breath of fresh air . . . a tonic . . . a stiff morning walk. It

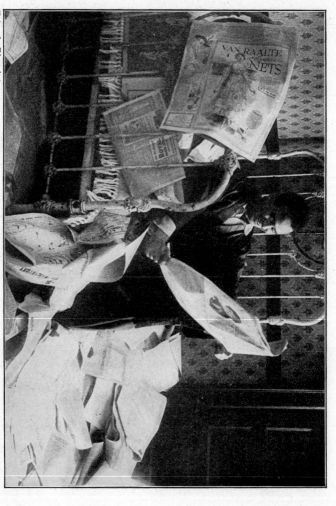

Triangle-Fine-Arts

A Scene from "His Picture in the Papers"

stirs the mind to action and inspires us to lift ourselves out of the rut into which we have fallen. One returns to them time after time, each reading opening up new vistas of thought, new lines of mental development.

As a man's stomach is what he eats, a man's mind is what he reads. It goes without saying that no healthy, active mind could exist without the companionship of Shakespeare. Nowadays it is possible to secure the entire works of the immortal poet in one volume. There is a special Oxford University edition which can be had for a small sum. The type is large, the paper good and there are many notes to help one over the rocky places. There is no doubt of the truth of the saying that a man who reads Shakespeare consistently and with understanding needs no other education. Like the philosopher Emerson he boiled down the world's thoughts into terse sentences and one goes into a new universe when reading any of the plays. It is a good thing to learn parts of them by heart so that we can apply them to our own lives. They strengthen the mind . . . their beauty lifts us into a great realism of splendid thought . . . and they fill the heart with a longing to do something great. Such books should become steady companions through life. No matter where our duties call us we should see to it that we do not leave behind the thoughts of this master mind of Shakespeare. The very fact that we have them near us lifts us out of the monotony of nothing to do.

Among the books about America for Americans perhaps Roosevelt's "Winning of the West" is among the best. Not only has he thrown the whole vigor of his interesting personality into the writing of it, but he has given us a vivid picture of the conquest of the States by the settlers. No man could read it without being thrilled at the dangers our forefathers faced . . . at the great courage they possessed . . . at their hardihood . . . their bulldog tenacity. The reading of such a book is like going back over the years and living with them, sharing their troubles and their enthusiasms. The man who contemplates gathering a small library could not afford to do without the inspiration of what his countrymen have done for him.

In choosing our books we must bear in mind one thing—*let them be inspiring*. Let them be of such a nature that when we read them we will feel like going out into the world to accomplish something *big!*

That is probably the mission of great books—to inspire and uplift. The world's greatest men have been readers—would they have cared for books unless they were inspiring? It is said that when Napoleon was being taken to St. Helena he advised one of the officers never to stop reading.

Most of the things worth while are at some time or other stored away in books by the thinkers. Every phase of history, every movement to better mankind and lift it above the drudgery of mere toil, every beautiful thought is to be found in them and the better the book the more will be found in it of these very things. When we have finished the day's work we can pull down a volume from the shelf and in a moment be lost in an entirely different world. The man who neglects to read surely misses the one best means of broadening his mind.

All books of the better class furnish food for thought and are excellent tools for the man of initiative. To read means keeping in touch with the big visions. We cherish these dreams and make them real in plans of our own. Aspiration is behind the pages of every worth-while volume. It was the motive power which drove the author to produce it and it should become a part of the forces which drive us on to victory. Without such inspiration we grope as children in the dark. We are without a light to guide us on our way.

Books by such men as Marden and Hubbard are great generators of the electricity of doing things. They have put into words those innermost emotions which are the instruments of success. They point out a way we may safely follow. They loan us inspiration which causes us to act for ourselves. They give us thoughts that are useful and practical which we never would have gained by virtue of our own reasoning power. They made it a life work to coin into phrases words that inspire. Out of their large experience came the logical sequences of cause and effect. Not to profit by their teachings is a crime against our own prospects—without them we lag behind. Instead of progressing we look on in wonder at what is going on in the world. Somehow we cannot connect ourselves with the big enterprises. And all because we failed to feed our minds properly.

There is much to be gained both in pleasure and knowledge by reading historical novels, and the lives of great men. The books of Sir Walter Scott and James Fenimore Cooper are rated among the best in the world. Grant's autobiography and the personal stories of other famous Americans provide fascinating material with which to establish and fortify our test for good literature. The tales of modern American financiers is another field of absorbing interest.

The man with small means can provide himself with a working library for a very little money. Books are cheap. The public library is always

nearby and there is hardly a town of any size but
what has one. When we purchase a book we
should be sure to obtain the best edition and be
careful that it is printed from good type and on
clear paper. Books are likely to become warm
friends. We should never purchase an abridged
edition.

Binding is not such an important factor,
although we like to have *our favorite books* put
up in a handsome fashion. With Shakespeare,
Emerson, Roosevelt, Scott, Cooper, Marden and
Hubbard one would have quite a representative
collection for a start. It would be easy to expand
the list into many more. Of course, those collect-
ing a small library who have a specialty, will want
books dealing with the subjects in which they are
interested. However, every practical library in-
cludes books of inspirational character, and if one
makes a study of the books written by great
authors it will be found that all of them profited
by the reading of books which caused them to
think. *The Bible causes us to think!—and no
library is complete without it.*

CHAPTER XII

PHYSICAL AND MENTAL PREPAREDNESS

It is not the object of this chapter to deal with a set course of physical culture, but rather to emphasize the necessity of keeping our physical house in order. There are plenty of books on physical culture which can be relied upon and also any number of physical instructors who are able to advise and help along a set program. There are hundreds of places, institutions, clubs, Y. M. C. A.'s, and the like, which provide gymnasiums and every other facility for those who determine to build themselves up through consistent physical exercise. That is all very well to begin with, but afterward we must have some simple methods of our own which will not make it a hardship or a chore to keep ourselves in trim —*a state of physical preparedness.* It should become a part of our daily scheme to obey certain, simple rules which tend toward an *automatic effort* instead of a discipline, and we should persevere in these until they become *fixed habits*.

It is no trouble at all to take exercise unconsciously, and we only arrive at this by turning into an exercise any of our ordinary physical actions during the day as we go along. For instance, we can sit down in a chair and in so doing can add a certain amount of exercise to the action itself—also in rising. With very little effort we can come into the habit of sitting correctly— posing the body as it should be—holding the shoulders in proper position—also the chin so that it becomes a hardship to sit improperly.

All of this has to do with *general physique*. In walking we can go along with a spring, elasticity, and vigor of motion which forces a fine blood circulation throughout the entire system. We can stoop over in the act of picking up some object from the floor and at the same time make it a matter of physical exercise, and we may take a hat from the rack while standing away from it, thus stretching ourselves, as it were, into a little needful action. Putting on an overcoat, or any part of our clothing, may be done in such a way as to set the blood to racing through the body. Morning and night—upon getting up and upon retiring—there is every reason to make it a rule to exercise freely.

The morning exercise wakes us up and sits us down finally at the breakfast table with a zest for the food set before us. The morning bath is an agency for good in this direction after we have given ourselves a good shake-up from head to foot. By the same token, exercises at night before retiring induces sound sleep and takes away the strain of the preceding day.

A very successful system is that of exercising in bed. Instead of immediately jumping to the floor in the morning it is very inviting to go through some simple form of gymnastics in which the physical structure is brought into play.

Physical exercise is something which can be carried to extremes. We can go at the work so intensely that we become muscle-bound and develop some structural enlargements that we do not need. This happens very often among athletes. The ordinary man should fight shy of such plans. Superfluous strength is only for those who have need of it. What we really want is strength enough to carry us through our daily rounds with comfort and *a feeling of efficiency*.

In a sense we all live by our wits and these decline when not properly fed by our general physical organization. Prize fighters are not the longest lived people, nor are the professional athletes. Their calling requires extra building up which would be a positive handicap to the average man whose manner of life doesn't require this super-development. In other words, there are intemperate methods of exercising just as there are of eating and drinking. We may easily go too far. Again, we can sin just as greatly by not going far enough. There was a time when men of forty were as worn and old as men of sixty-five and seventy are today. As a matter of fact, nowadays a half-century mark is no longer a badge of senility when a man has kept himself fit and treated himself right.

We all have friends who are pretty well along in years by virtue of their carefully planned physical training, plus their *cheerful dispositions.* They are as sprightly and companionable as though they were many years younger. We should come to know early in life what a large part *good humor* plays in *physical fitness.* In previous chapters hearty laughter was extolled as one of the very best of exercises. It is an organizer in itself and opens up the heart and lungs as nothing else will do. It makes the blood go galloping all through the system. It is one of the best automatic *blood circulators* in the business.

Laughter takes the stress off of the mind, and whatever is ahead of us for the day that seems likely to become a burden is soon turned into an ordinary circumstance. We smile as we go about doing it.

A friend once said to a banker:

"How do you know when to lend money?"

The banker replied:

"I look a man in the eye and then *I do or I don't*."

The friend said:

"I would like to borrow ten thousand dollars —now!"

"You shall have it, Sir," the banker replied.

This meant that the man who asked for the loan was in a state of physical and mental preparedness. If he had gone into the banker's office looking like an animated tombstone he wouldn't have had much of a chance to borrow the ten thousand. It goes without saying that the open-faced, hearty fellow inspires confidence. There is nothing coming to the dried-up, sour chap, and that's what he usually gets. And what we get is largely a matter of our physical well being. A modern philosopher observed that "the blues are the product of bad livers"—and there is no doubt but that he was right.

The problem of life is to fill our days with sunshine. In so doing we shall find that the "little graces" are those which will lend us the most help. Tiny favors extended, words of encouragement, courtesies of all sorts, unselfish work carried out in an open manner, true friendships and love, a hearty laugh, a sincere appreciation of the other fellow's struggle to keep his head above water, the conscientious carrying out of all tasks assigned us—these are our helpmates and they are the products of our physical and mental equipment. Through these we come into our knack of detecting friends among those who are *the salt of the earth.*

It is impossible for the person who desires good health to obtain it, or having it, to retain it, without consistent effort. A watch will not run without the proper regulation of the mainspring. We must keep up our activities. We have taken the earth and are turning it into something to serve us—therefore the need of fine bodily preparedness. Nothing can take the place of achievement and it comes through physical and mental efficiency. The one must not be neglected for the other; both must be cultivated and developed alike in order that each may help the other.

Happiness comes only to those who take care

of themselves. It is the natural product of *clean-mindedness*. No pleasure can surpass that of a conscious feeling of our strength of character. It is an all important element in men who aspire to succeed. The man who rises in the morning from a healthy slumber and plunges into the bath after some vigorous exercise is prepared to undertake anything. His world seems fair, and though the sun may not be shining literally, it is to all intents and purposes. Thus, we go swinging along with a cheery smile, carrying the message of hope and joy to all those with whom we come in contact. Oh! it's fine to be physically and mentally fit!

CHAPTER XIII

SELF-INDULGENCE AND FAILURE

The correct definition of self-indulgence is *failure*—because self-indulgence is comprised of an aggregation of vices, large and small, and failure is the logical sequence thereof. Even the habit of eating may be cultivated into a vice. Indeed, there are those who gorge without restraint, which in itself is unchaste and immoral. We've often seen them as, with napkin under foot or tucked under the collar, they eat their way through mountains of food and wash it down as they reach for more.

No use to say how and what we feel when we attend such performances. It is all right to say "Look the Other Way," *but it can't be done.* It is human nature to gaze upon horror—sometimes in sympathy, but more often in amazement. Sometimes a well staged scene of gormandizing viewed from a seat in the second or third row center of a softly lighted, thick carpeted food emporium *saves us the price of our own meal.* We no longer hunger on our own account. Our appetite is appeased by proxy, so to speak, and we calmly fix our eyes on the "big show" and *sigh for a baseball bat.*

No wonder a noted bachelor of medicine declares "People are what they eat!" The exclamation point is our own. We quite agree with our medical brother for we have seen people eat until we thought *we* would never be hungry again.

But there is more to self-indulgence than the food specialist has to answer for, so we will be on our way. For instance, there is *the spend-thrift;* surely he is entitled to a short stanza. We all know him. He goes on the theory that he has all the spending money in the world, and that long after he is dead those on whom he spent it will remember his generosity. Vain hope!— Whatever memory of him remains will be of a different kind. Those who have been bored by

Triangle-Fine-Arts

Douglas Fairbanks in "The Good Bad-Man"

his gratuitous attentions will take up the threads of their existence where they left off when he drove them away from their usual haunts. No longer will they have to dodge down alleys and run up strange stairways in an effort to avoid his overtures.

When alive and in full operation he knew more about what was best for us than we could possibly think of knowing. Left to his own devices he would have us smoke his particular brands, drink his labels, eat his selections, wear his kind of a cravat, overcoat, cap, hat, shoes, and underwear. And to make his proposition sound business like he would willingly pay the bills! In this little amusement we are supposed to play the part of receiver and *praise his generosity.*

Whatever may be our verdict on this chap we must keep in mind that his inordinate desire to waste his substance was no less than a vice if for no other reason than its example upon others; it is just as bad to be *a "receiver"* as it is to be *a spendthrift.* If we cannot build up a reputation for generosity without becoming ostentatious we might better take lessons in refinement from someone "to the manor born."

There is no desire to single out and set down by name and number every sort of self-indulgence. *Excesses of any kind are indulgences,* and it is easy to fall into them if we have not built up our stamina to resist.

Our failures are usually traceable to ourselves. No matter what excuses may be offered in our behalf we know in our own minds that we are to blame. Somewhere along the line of our endeavors we faltered—*then we fell.* Our conservatism reinforced by our strength of character finally gave way at a given point and put the whole plant out of business. Our system of inspection had become cursory instead of painstaking. Everything had been running along so smoothly we forgot that everything *must* wear out in time if it isn't looked after properly.

A previous chapter entitled, "Taking Stock of Ourselves," has a specific bearing upon the subject in hand. It emphasizes the necessity of taking stock of ourselves early in life in order that we may know our weak spots and take immediate steps to dig them out by the roots and replace them with *"hardy perennials,"* which thrive on and on unto the last day.

And that reminds us that it is well to take stock of ourselves every little while. Even "hardy perennials" have to be looked after—the ground kept fertile and watered against the draughts of forgetfulness and neglect. And so it must be with our mental and physical processes in order that each day of our lives we may go forth with renewed forcefulness—with every atom of character in full working order.

Having started off on the right foot, we are less likely to have trouble with our higher resolves during the lean and hungry years of our youth when we go plunging headlong toward the goal of our ambitions. Usually it is not until we come into "Easy Street" that we find that we dropped something somewhere along the line which we must replace at once or we will be laid up for repairs. But lo and behold! "Easy Street" is fair to look upon. It dazzles the eye—it takes hold of the sensibilities. Everybody wears "Sunday clothes" on this street and seems to be superlatively happy. Surely it wouldn't hurt to linger awhile and see what is going on. Why, this is the most talked about street in the world! Some of the people we have dealt with have told us about it. They said it was *the only street* for a man of means, for there could be found the very things for which we strive in life. They told us that the people we would meet represented the higher order of intelligence, brainy, alert, accomplished—a grand thoroughfare for those who would know life in the fullness thereof.

Now it is a fact that "Easy Street" may be crossed and recrossed in safety every day of our lives if we do not tarry. Financial competence might permit of it, but competent efficiency demands that we trot along—*keep moving*—get away before we settle down into its ways. The action we need is not along this brilliant lane.

But suppose we do take a chance just to test the serene confidence which we think is so safely nailed down within us. The very thought

of it makes the "caution bell" tinkle in our ears
—but caution is a species of cowardice, after all,
we say—a man of *courage* may dare anything
once.   And just at the moment we waver who
comes along but our old friend *Self-indulgence!*
—the well dressed, carefree fellow who once told
us all about "Easy Street" and invited us to look
in on him sometime.   Nothing would please him
more than to show us the whole works—and here
he is shaking us by the hand and pulling us along
—for he is an affable fellow and will not take
"no" for an answer.

Our struggle is feeble—a huge chunk of our
strength of character falls off into space then and
there.   Even at the gilded entrance we try again to
beg off—to slip away—but Self-indulgence will
not hear. So together we go through the portals
leading into a grandeur we had never known—beyond our experience and power to believe. *This is
likely to become the turning point in our career.*

Bill Nye once said "When we start down hill
we usually find everything greased for the occasion."   We might add—*"except the bumps!"*

CHAPTER XIV

LIVING BEYOND OUR MEANS

Living beyond our means is a big subject that must be treated broadly, for circumstances alter cases. There is a sane way to look at every problem, and the matter of living beyond our means is one of the major problems we have to face. If every man was alike and every avocation in life was on a parity, it would be possible to dispose of this subject in a paragraph. But men are not alike. What one could do successfully might easily baffle another. Therefore, it seems advisable to consider the subject by looking into its depths.

To most people debt is terrifying. To some it means nothing—and thus we have individual temperament as an angle from which to consider. Living beyond our ability to pay means going into debt via the shortest route. Getting out of debt means a revision of our code to the extent of ceasing to live beyond our means and saving something with which to pay off what we owe. Some men can do this successfully—others fail while seemingly trying their best to succeed— and still others do nothing to stem the tide. With these it is a matter of how the tide serves. If favoring winds should drive them to opulence they would more than likely pay up, particularly those imbued with *sufficient personal honor* to "make good."

Such are the exigencies of life, we may as well concede that a vast majority at some time or other find it necessary to owe more than they can readily pay. Emergencies arise which force us into expenses that require credit, and if we have so ordered our lives that when the pinch comes *we have no credit established* the fact that we pay out our last dollar and go hungry to bed does not bring us much sympathy. Thus it would seem that to be able to say: "I pay as I go," or, "I owe no man a dollar," or, "I never live beyond my means" is not much of a boast, when, after a death in the family, or other unforeseen circumstances, we find ourselves broke and nowhere to turn for accommodation.

It has been aptly said that *"People can save themselves to death."* In other words, one may develop the saving habit to such an extent that "Laugh and Live" can find no room beside us on the perch of our existence. We must admit that the systematic saver of pennies misses a lot as he goes along, and, with time, degenerates into a sort of "Kill Joy." In the matter of regulating his family to his way of thinking he usually has an uphill job. Sons leave home as soon as they can; daughters marry and breathe a sigh of relief, leaving mother behind to slave on *in order that the hoard may grow.*

While all of this is true it only represents extreme cases, therefore it should not be construed that this chapter is launched against *the habit of saving.* Rather, its purpose is to suggest the thought of not *"over-saving"* at the expense of *personal welfare.* Our best plan would be to save in reason, not forgetting that life is here to

Squaring Things With Sister—From "The Habit of Happiness"

enjoy as we go along. Then, too, we must have a *credit rating* among our fellow mortals, just the same as a business person must have credit rating among financial institutions.

Credit in business is worth more than money because it allows for expansion whereas money in the bank is only good *as far as it goes*. Many a merchant who bought and sold for cash all his life found when he came to enlarge his business that one thing was lacking—*credit*. The fact that he had always paid cash threw a doubt upon his financial condition when he proposed to borrow. He had neglected to build up a credit as he went along. The business world only knew him as a man who paid cash and exacted cash. Taken at his fullest inventory he had "scalped" a living out of the world for which he had done but little to make happier or better. One calamity might easily scuttle his prospects forever—for instance, a fire, or a bank failure. And without credit it would be difficult to start over again.

By all means we must save something for the "rainy day" as we go along—and our savings can be made up of other things than actual cash in bank. One item of our savings is the habit of *keeping up our appearances*. Living beyond our means does not incorporate the thought that, in order to save every possible cent, we should become slipshod and shabby. Carelessness in dress takes away from our rating as nothing else will for it has to do with first impressions of those with whom we come in contact. Gentility pays dividends of the highest order, being, as it is, a badge of character. Neatness *bespeaks character,* and it is just as cheap in dollars and cents to keep ourselves respectably clothed as to indulge in shoddy apparel under the delusion that we have saved money on the purchase price. Good clothing, costing more at the start, lasts long *and looks well as long as it lasts*. Shoddy apparel never is anything else but shoddy, and well might it proclaim the shoddy man.

When we throw away our opportunity to present a genteel appearance, just for the sake of the bank roll, we doom ourselves to defeat in the pursuit of knowledge. We cannot get all we want to know by the mere reading of books. We must mingle with people; we must interchange thought that we may crystallize what we know into practical knowledge so it can be made into tools to work with. While a man of brains is welcome everywhere the matter of his appearance has a lot to do with how he is received and with whom he may fraternize.

"Isn't it a pity," we hear people say, "that, with all his brains, he hasn't sense enough to make himself presentable?" But the worst phase of the situation is that the unkempt man sooner or later loses faith in himself and either ceases to hoard at the expense of his gentility or he gives up his opportunity to mingle with others and lapses into habits consistent with miserly thoughts.

The phrase *"a happy medium"* is well known and decidedly applicable to the subject of saving as we go along so that we may avert the sorrows which follow in the wake of *living beyond our means*. It suggests a desirable middle course which permits us to adopt a sane policy, rather than flying to an extreme.

It cannot be said that we are living beyond our means when by reason of our association with men of affairs we need to spend more money and thereby save less in preparing ourselves for the larger opportunities which will naturally follow. Young men often go through college on their "uppers," so to speak. There is not a cent which they could honestly save as they went along without cheating themselves. The point is that their situations in life force them to spend rather than to save money. But in so doing the real saving was in the spending thereof. *They enlarged their knowledge and decreased their bank accounts for the time being.* What man parts with in an emergency is no license, however, for him to fall back into profligacy. Never should a man entirely lose the idea of putting something by. The college boy in this case has simply invested his money in an education instead of a bank account.

Once on the highroad of life with a plan of

action well defined and a regular income *the habit of putting money away should become a fixed procedure.* In no other way do we accumulate except by investment, and investment means putting away money at interest or in some project which promises better returns.

If we were to interview a thousand men on the subject of saving and draw upon their experiences we would find that by investing money at interest we pursue the safest course, far safer, in fact, than the seeking of outside investments that *promise* greater returns. The latter invites the mind away from the regular avocation and educates it in time to *take chances* that are likely to turn into *setbacks.* The mind, instead of applying itself to the duty of making the most out of its regular employment, allows its interest to become scattered over too broad a field.

It is not within the province of all men to become wealthy and, after all, wealth is not the only desideratum; the happiest of mortals are found in the middle walks of life and not in the extremes. The struggle should be to escape the life which saps our strength, keeps our nerves on edge and drives us away from the *green pastures.*

CHAPTER XV

INITIATIVE AND SELF-RELIANCE

The late Elbert Hubbard defined the man with initiative as the one who did the right thing at the right time without being told. At this point it may be definitely stated that such a man would naturally be *self-reliant*. Such a man would not lean on his friends. He would *stand up* with them. . . . He would be found fighting his own battles without crying for help.

Once a cub reporter was ordered by his city editor to go and interview a certain man. After an awkward pause the youngster inquired: "Where can I find him?" Smiling scornfully into his eyes the city editor replied: "Wherever he is."

This would seem to have been the start and finish of this youngster's newspaper career, but quite the reverse was true. He took the lesson well to heart, thus starting himself on the road

125

to self-reliance. If he had repeated the offense it is likely he would have lost his job and also *his nerve*—thereby spoiling his chances for a successful career. The fact that he did not, but went on and made of himself a famous newspaper man, proves that he lost no time in developing *initiative and self-reliance.*

There is no questioning the vast importance these two words mean to all of us. Many a man who did not grasp the significance of initiative became a *"leaner"* for the rest of his life. Many a man also missed his chances by doing *just as he was told* and nothing more. His work ended there. In due course it is inevitable that such a man should become part of the great army of discontented ne'er-do-wells who help to block the pavements in front of the loafing places.

Hesitation, vacillation and growing diffidence take the place of self-reliance. He falls to the bottom like a stone. And there he rests—a drag anchor in the mire. His job gets the best of him because he lacks initiative. Once stranded he

A Scene from "In Again—Out Again"

becomes an arrant coward—*afraid of his own shadow*.

We must *make our own opportunities* otherwise we are children of circumstance. What becomes of us is a matter of guesswork. We have no hand in compelling our own future. *Diffidence is a species of cowardice.* It causes a man's courage to ooze out at his toes faster than it comes into his heart. *Such men often have big ideas, but having no confidence in themselves they lack the power to compel confidence in others.* When they go into the presence of a man of personality they lose their self-confidence and all of the pent-up courage which drove them forward flies out at the window. Their weakness multiplies with each failure until finally "the jig is up" —*their impotency is complete.*

Very largely those who have big ideas to present expect to be taken in on them and to be given an opportunity to succeed along with their scheme. When a man becomes so unfortunate as to be unable through diffidence to explain himself, his big idea goes into the waste basket and with it all of the hopes he has built upon it. *Another nail has been driven into his casket of failures.*

To such a man, all pity, but we will not allow him to escape until we have given him a pat on the back and pointed out the right road to travel. We mustn't preach to him or undertake to force him to do anything, but we will at least give him a helping hand and show him that there is *a royal road to his goal.*

This man needs first of all to build upon his physique. Perhaps he has a *bad stomach,* and likewise *bad teeth.* Exercise—regular exercise, should be the first thing on his program. Fresh air, long walks, deep breathing, dumb bells, boxing, rowing, skating in season—*and wholesome companionship day by day.* In the long run boxing will become his most efficient exercise. When a man can take a blow between the eyes and come back for more he has begun to *fortify his own combativeness.* That is what he needs in life's battles—the nerve to *come back for more* after a slam on the jaw that would lay another man low. And when it's all said and done and the exercise game has become a feature of his day's work, he must settle down to *good plain food and plenty of sleep.* There is nothing in all the world like these things combined for the upbuilding and upholding of health and courage.

Our success is a matter of our courage. A man who can steel himself to be knocked down and get up immediately afterwards and hand the other fellow a ripping punch has added to his own "pep." *All courage is of the same cloth, whether physical, moral or spiritual.* To build upon one is to build up the others—the human system being constructed on such a basis that if one part is affected all the rest follow suit.

A man who isn't afraid of a physical combat will readily match his wits with his fellow man. Physical training is therefore all important to *initiative and self-reliance.*

Our natural aim is to make for ourselves a true personality that does not know defeat. When we come to an obstacle we must be able to hurdle it. It is all very well to say that the longest way around is the shortest way across, but it doesn't sound like initiative and self-reliance. There is one thing about men who rely upon themselves— they make no excuses, nor do they puff up over victory.

Posing for applause is as distasteful to them as standing for abuse. All they ask is a square deal and the confidence of their associates. If they fall down on a proposition they get up and go at it again until success crowns their efforts. Such men have a way of *turning defeat into victory*.

How immeasurably inferior to such a spirit is the fellow who whines and moans at every evil twist of fortune. He has no confidence in himself and nothing else to do except confide his woes to all who will listen to his cowardly story of defeat. Such men are least useful in the important work of this world. They are the humdrum hirelings—the dumb followers. The pitiful part of it all is that they could have succeeded had they but taken stock of themselves when the taking was good. But while there is life there is hope—likewise a chance. *It is up to us.*

One of the startling things about men of initiative is the way they come forward in times of trouble. We don't have to point to Andrew Jackson in the War of 1812. We can look around us. Take, for example, a great fire. Haven't we often read of the brave fireman who sprang forward and by doing the right thing instantly, saved a multitude of lives? Well, such a man is possessed of self-reliance. He is trained for the hazardous life he leads. When the emergency arose he was ready in a jiffy to do the work expected of him.

It is safe to say that without training such men would have botched the job and instead of being praised to the skies would have sunk into oblivion under the heap of public scorn. Sometimes it happens that a man accidentally becomes a hero, but it was no accident that he was *able to become one*. He must have had initiative—he must have had self-reliance. Archibald C. Butt was such a man. He went down on the *Titanic*. The last act of his life was to help women and children into the boats and calm their minds as they were lowered away. Astor was of the same metal—*both sublimely oblivious to the terrible fate which hung over them.* Here was initiative and self-reliance in its highest form.

And this sort of man is everywhere. The car in which we ride to work every morning contains one or more of them. Let something happen and we will see them spring forward with a line of action already formed. At their word of command we automatically obey—and then when the worst is over a kindly voice reassures us and we go on our way rejoicing.

What would the world do without these men? History is filled with the tales of heroes and heroines. And for every Joan of Arc there are thousands upon thousands who have done heroic things without a word of praise. Moreover, the really brave soul declines all ovation. No real hero claims reward. *To have done the right thing at the right time is reward in itself.*

This quality of self-strength and self-dependence is not confined to any race of people, but in nations where personal liberty survives initiative is at its best. Somehow, whenever the emergency, *the man comes forth to do and dare*. The great world war, still raging as these lines are penned, has furnished untold thousands of examples of courageous action—enough to last until the end of human affairs, but they will go on and on in multiplied form, each day's score superseding those of the day before. It would be bully to know that we are doing our share in *safeguarding the supply* of Initiative and Self-reliance needed in this world.

We must keep moving. The fellow who gets in a rut through lack of initiative finds that with advancing years it becomes harder and harder to get out of it, so that the best plan is to make the move now while there is time to succeed. When we come to think of it, there are plenty of positions in the world for the right man, and if we have something to say for ourselves that lends credit to our ability we stand a chance for the job.

CHAPTER XVI

FAILURE TO SEIZE OPPORTUNITIES

There is an old saying to the effect that "opportunity knocks but once at our door"—and that is all *fol de rol*. Opportunity knocks at some people's doors nearly every day of their lives and is given a royal welcome. That's what Opportunity likes—*appreciation*. It goes often to the home where the latchstring hangs on the outside. It's like a sign reading "Hot coffee at all hours, day or night"—very inviting. Very much different, however, from the abode whose windows shed no light and whose door *is barred from within*.

"Nobody Home!" that's the sign for this door. Mister Numbskull lives here and most of the time *he sleeps*. When anyone knocks on his door he pulls the covers up over his head to shut out the noise. He's down on his luck anyhow, therefore it would be a waste of good shoe leather for him to be up and puttering around. If Opportunity ever knocked at his door he could say in all truth that *he never heard it*. He had often heard of Opportunity being in the neighborhood, but one thing is certain—*someone else had invariably seen him first*. He felt sure he would know Opportunity if ever he met him face to face, and if ever he did he would have it out with him then and there.

Meanwhile—dadgast the luck!—always the fates pursued him with some sort of hoodoo. And his neighbors—well, some of them had sense enough to keep their distance and let him alone. Others, however, had not been considerate of the fact that a "Jinx" was on his trail, and were given to making sarcastic remarks concerning him. And thus it was that Mister Numbskull spent his days, dodging his neighbors, sidestepping the highways and obscuring himself from the very individual he wanted so much to behold—*Opportunity*. At last there came a time when, in despair, *and in disrepute,* he took to the woods and

is yet to be heard from. Opportunity still visits
the neighborhood, but the path leading to Mister
Numbskull's home is grown up in weeds.

The fact is that our real opportunity *knocks
from within.* Through experience, built upon
consecutively by continuous effort, our vision ex-
pands and pounds its way out through the portals of our brain. We see the thing that we ought
to do and *we go to it!* To the man who didn't see
it *the opportunity did not exist.*

"What we don't know doesn't hurt us any"—
so runs the old saw. And here's a case where we
who didn't see, *were* hurt, but we didn't know it.

For those of us who have vision there are all
sorts of opportunities, but many of them are not
good for us. The ones we make for ourselves are
the healthy ones, and generally they are the best
for us. "Our own baby" is the one we will take
the greatest pride in and enjoy the most. Then
we become masters of our own destiny in a sense
and can be more independent through having no
senior partners in the enterprise. Often our
dreams bring forth a need for many kinds of

special knowledge and for these we go into the open market offering opportunity to many others in return for their assistance. Thus we find that everything we do is in relation to other things and dependent in part on other people.

This should make us careful and a wee bit wary. Opportunities are widely divergent in nature—through a stroke of hard luck one might have difficulty in finding employment. The first opportunity might lead to a job in a bar-room, but having fortified ourselves by developing our highest attributes such as honesty, integrity, cleanliness of body and mind—we are able to somehow or other pinch along until something better shows itself. First-class principles are not to be thrown away upon the first provocation, therefore, in order to take away the temptation, we might as well figure out that a great many employments in the world do not represent *real opportunities* and therefore should not be considered.

Failure to seize such so-called opportunities becomes a virtue in the same sense that the failure to seize a decent opportunity becomes a shame.

Often opportunity comes through meeting men of affairs who have power and wealth at their command. These are usually in connection with enterprises of the greater magnitude. Those of us who have the power to control our destinies to a reasonable degree should not stand back in our support of these. If we have carefully built up our initiative, self-reliance, preparedness in the way of efficiency, good health and the will to do, there is no reason why we should not aspire to take a hand in anything in which we are confident we can succeed. Among the men who control the big affairs of the business world we find a true democracy— *they want the man*. The fact that he appears before them neatly attired, bright of eye and ready of wit will surely count in his favor.

In other words, we should live up to the opportunity in whatever form it presents itself after we have accepted its responsibilities. To make this perfectly plain *we must live up to the job!* If we are to be superintendent of a coal mine "underneath the ground" we will put on our overalls and jumpers, but if we are to be manager of a grand opera house we will appear in our dress suits. The thought is obvious, but as we journey along we find many of our fellow mortals neglecting to live in line with what they are doing.

We mention this fact hopeful that we will not fail to seize our opportunities by setting up obstacles whereby we may become *persona non grata* through lack of discernment.

Opportunity is within ourselves and when we have seized our rightful share, then we may look with pride upon our endeavor and proceed to *laugh and live!*

CHAPTER XVII

ASSUMING RESPONSIBILITIES

Those who fear to assume responsibility necessarily *take orders from others*. The punishment fits the crime perfectly and being self-inflicted there is no injustice. It is true that many men possessed of great brain power play "second fiddle" to shallow-minded men of inferior wisdom from sheer lack of forcefulness on their own part. They lack the full quality of leadership while possessing all save one essential—*courage*. Fear abides in their hearts and spreads itself as a mantle of gloom over their super-sensitive souls until finally they struggle no more. Henceforth they are doomed and become the subject of apology on the part of friends and relations. He's all right," they say, "but he suffers from over-refinement. He lacks something—we cannot make out just what. It is altogether too bad for he is such a superior man among *his social equals.*

We must take our hats off to those who have the goodness of heart to make allowance for our shortcomings. A disinterested listener, however, is seldom taken into camp by such well intended argument. He knows that "friend husband" or "friend brother" as the case may be, needs some sort of swift kick that will stir his combativeness into action—that will cause him to turn upon his mental inferior and have it out with him then and there—once and for all. As a courage builder *fighting for justice* is not to be sneezed at.

Courage can be built up just the same as any other soul quality. It is all a matter of early training as to which we start out with—courage or fear. Unthinking parents have a lot to do with the propagation of fear in the hearts of children. A *neglectful father* plus a *fear-stricken mother* constitute the most logical forces which tend toward the overdevelopment of fear in a child. Once the seed is thoroughly implanted the growth can be depended upon. How to get rid of it later is not so easy to figure out. Had the child been born with a "clubfoot" these same parents would have spent their last dollar in an effort to straighten it into natural condition. They could see the unshapely foot day by day with their own eyes—and so could their neighbors. But the fear-warped little brain struggling for courage with which to combat its weakness needs must battle alone with chances largely against it.

The mere thought of what is in store for this little one as it stumbles along from one period to another, fearful of this, and fearful of that, is disconcerting to say the least. We can almost trace our friend "Second Fiddle" directly back to such a childhood. We can almost hear his fond mother shout, "Keep away from the brook, darling, you might get your feet wet and *catch your death of a cold.*" Another well known and highly respected admonition belonging to childhood's hour is, "Come in, deary, it's getting dark

Bungalowing in California

—Bogie man will get you if you don't watch out."

Some years later when little son runs breathless into the home portal after being chased from school by some "turrible" boys we can hear this same little mother as she storms about the place and tells what "papa must do" about the matter. According to her notion, if teachers could not control the "criminal element" among their pupils then it was high time for the police to step in. Never a word about little son taking his own part! Father listens in silence and half formulates the notion of going direct to the parents and laying down the law, while little son listens in fear and trembling in anticipation of what is coming to him if father carries out his threat.

Tall oaks from little acorns grow—*if the twig is not bent in the sprouting.*

Little son is bound to grow into manhood some day and when he arrives he must have one particular attribute—*courage.* Somehow he will get along if he has that. He may also wear a "clubfoot" or a "hunch back," but with courage as a running mate he will assume his responsibilities and become a force in the world.

Once a great orator sat upon a rostrum listening to a speech by a man who cautioned his countrymen against taking steps to defend the national honor. "We'll outlive the taunts of those who would drag us into war!" he bellowed forth. Whereupon the orator jumped to his feet and with clarion voice shouted, "God hates a coward!" and then sat down again.

Dazed at first the vast throng sat stupefied—but only for a moment. Then as one man they jumped to their feet and by reason of prolonged cheering gave national impulse to a thought which has since been sermonized from thousands of pulpits. The orator had simply paraphrased and put "pep" into the old Biblical slogan: "The Lord helps those who help themselves." The effect was electrical. The whole country rallied to the idea with the result that we saved ourselves from war by showing the solid front of being ready and willing to defend ourselves.

Everything that tends to build up courage is

an asset in life. The more we have of it the further we go and the more interesting our lives become. For *the man of the lion heart* all things unfold and unto him the timid must bring their offerings. No one of ordinary gumption consults the human "flivver." Advice from him would be unavailing. His point of view would be inadequate—his ability to advise, impotent. We go to the man who does things and say to him: "Here is my little idea—do you want to help me put it over?" If it is good, he does. If not, his experience tells him so, for men of courage are naturally possessed of large vision. Their lack of fear has given them right-of-way over vast areas of the world of action. They fail only as "their lights go out forever."

With courage we order our own lives and take orders only from those of superior wisdom. This we can never afford *not to do*. The courageous man of largest vision commands by his power to reason logically and therefore assumes the air of comradeship rather than "overseer" or "boss."

Only through lack of moral and physical courage are we to become the slaves of these.

Courage—the child of *Hope—the despair of Failure*. Born of Good Cheer it links its fate with the higher attributes and tramples under foot the fears which spring up before it. When *sown early* into the hearts of the young its companionship becomes unerring in its efficiency for good throughout their lives.

CHAPTER XVIII

WEDLOCK IN TIME

It is a happy idea to marry while we are young —a fine thing—a good thing—*a pleasant duty indeed* to marry the woman of our choice at a time of life when both are at an age when adjustment is natural and lasting loyalties are implanted in our hearts and minds for all time. We make a sad mistake when we postpone so important a step just for the sake of becoming a rich man first so that our bride-to-be may step into luxurious quarters and never have to lift her dainty hands except to sip from the glass of nectar we have set before her. The real facts compiled by the statistical "System Sams" are against this idea. The balance comes up in red ink *on the wrong side of the ledger.*

According to these gentlemen the average mortal is likely to be very fat and much over forty

147

before he can make an offering according to his first generous impulses and the chances are he will never reach the goal in this life. By the time he might be financially ready there is a hard glint in his eye, and he will be looking for the mote in the eye of his lady love. The waiting game is a hard one *and it makes us worldly*. After the lapse of years what once seemed a *rose* might appear to be more of a *hollyhock*.

Naturally we never blame ourselves for the changes. Had we obeyed the grand impulse in the hour of our youth we might have kept the garden full of roses and the hollyhocks would never have sprouted there. Then the home nest would have tinged our sensibilities with its loveliness and our affections would have been nailed down hard and fast *forever and a day*.

Among the many baffling problems which the young man faces, and for that matter, any man, is marriage. More thought, more energy and more time is taken up over this one decisive step than over any other. The reasons are obvious. It involves for life the happiness of the contracting parties—not only in a direct and personal way, but also in a general sense. The man's business success largely depends upon the helpmate he has in his home. *His career is at her mercy.* For example, if the wife should turn out to be unsympathetic, and uninterested in his ambitions, this fact might warp his prospects by causing him to *lose heart* in facing the large problems awaiting him along the road of opportunity. However, if she is of a cheerful, energetic disposition and willing to do all that she can to help him over the rough spots as they travel along together he will be *inspired into action* and will do his level best. He will be conscious as he goes about his work that there is *one* person above all upon whom he can depend—*his wife.*

Marriage is a *serious business* and usually we concede that point in the beginning. However, this is not aimed as a blow at life's greatest romance . . . it is merely the recognition of an elemental fact. . . . Marriage must have its *practical side.* To become successful in the highest degree man and wife *must establish a com-*

radeship. It is not the part of wisdom that either should rule the other, but rather that each should have the interest of the other at heart and should strive to be helpful one unto the other. Two men can go through life the best of friends, each holding the respect and confidence of the other. So can two women. *Then, why not a man and wife?* Needless to say they can, and do. Such partnerships are sure of success. It is only through lack of comradeship that love flies out of the window—*and lights on a sea-going aeroplane.*

The marriage state is a long contract—it should not be stumbled into by man or woman. Nor should we become cowardly to the point of backing out of it altogether. Love is blind *only to the blind.* Either party to the tie that binds has a chance to know in advance whether the venture is safe and sane. All a man has to consider after he knows his own heart is that the woman of his choice is sensible, considerate and healthy. Other things being equal he can take the leap without hesitancy. We shouldn't borrow trouble.

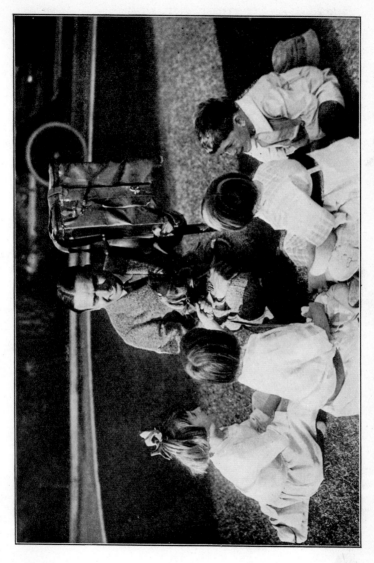

Demonstrating the Monk and the Hand-Organ to a Body of Psychologists

Of course there are those who *should never marry*. They do, however, and when they do they loan themselves to the mockery of the marriage state. There is no time to dwell on this thought for it is just something that goes on happening anyway and has no bearing upon the advisability of "wedlock in time" between *people of horse sense*.

Given a good wife, after his own heart, no manly man has a righteous kick coming against the fates. Under such circumstances if things go wrong he will find the fault within himself. Of course we should, to the fullest possible extent, be prepared for marriage before assuming its responsibilities. We should at least have a ticket before embarking—and it is the *real* man's duty to provide the ticket. Since it is to be a long voyage a "round trip" isn't necessary. In other words, a man needn't be rich when he marries—but he should not be broke, either. Lack of funds a few days after the honeymoon is too hard a test for matrimony to bear nobly. It is too much like inviting a catastrophe through lack of good, hard sense to begin with. It shows poor generalship at the very start—and there is the liability of causing great distress and hardship to a tender-hearted little woman. It would be a sad blow to her to find that the man of her choice was, after all, just an ordinary fellow—*a man without foresight*.

There are four seasons in married life—spring, summer, fall and winter, and we are going to need a comrade as we go through each of them. And the one we want *is the one we start with*— the gentle partner in all our joys and sorrows. It is she who will stand back of us when all others fail. When the children come along to bless our days and inspire us to greater efforts we are glad to look into their happy, smiling faces and find that they resemble their mother—their soft cheeks are like hers, their hands, their dainty ways, their caresses. And when mama looks into those same bright eyes they make her think of their daddy. The fond affection bestowed upon the children by both parents is but another mode of expressing their regard for each other.

Springtime days, these! When little tots climb up and entwine their arms about our necks. If this were married life's only compensation it would not prove in vain—for when the babies enter the home the tie that binds becomes hard and fast—*if the man is a manly man.* To become the father of a bright-eyed babe is an experience of the highest importance to a young man getting started. It reinforces his courage, doubles up his ambitions and *puts him on his metal.* He has a new responsibility and it adds to his strength of character to assume it in all its phases. Another thing it brings comfort and joy to the mother during the long days while her man is out in the fray. *It drives ennui out of the household throughout our springtime days.*

And when summer comes along new hopes dawn within us. Springtime had found us up and doing and when it merged into the new season we found our aspirations even stronger than before. Children must be educated and their futures prepared in advance as far as may be. They must not go into the world *without tools to work with.* Meanwhile the household teems with plans and becomes a veritable dreamland of youthful fervor. We find that having helped our children into attractive personalities they have become magnets with which to draw about us their comrades. Thus we hold on to our youth by virtue of our surroundings—creatures of our thoughtfulness concerning *"wedlock in time."*

That the fall season is coming has no terrors for us. There will be the weddings and plannings for new homes *close by*—if we have our say. And in due course, the grandchildren will come who will favor grandpa and grandma and once again youth knocks at our door. There will be no dread winter days for us for we have been forehanded—we have a *new crew on board to chase away the cares of old age and infirmities.*

Try how we will there is no way to forestall the operation of the law of compensation. We reap as we sow. The world will be good to those who compel its respect by becoming the right sort of citizens. *Wedlock in time—that's the answer!*

CHAPTER XIX

LAUGH AND LIVE

Again I find it expedient to resort to the personal pronoun and therefore this final chapter is to be devoted to *"you* and *me."* There are facts you may want to know *for sure* and one of them is whether or not I live up to my own prescription.

I do—*and it's easy!*

I have kept myself happy and well through keeping my physical department in first class order. If that had been left to take care of itself I would surely have fallen by the wayside in other departments. Once we sit down in security the world seems to *hand us things we do not need.*

Fresh air is my intoxicant—and it keeps me in high spirits. My system doesn't crave artificial stimulation because *my daily exercise*

155

quickens the blood sufficiently. Then, too, I manage to *keep busy*. That's the real elixir— *activity!* Not always physical activity, either, for I must read good books in order to exercise my mind in other channels than just my daily routine—and add to my store of knowledge as well.

Then there is my *inner-self* which must have attention now and then. For this a little solitude is helpful. We have only to sense the phenomena surrounding us to know that we must have a *working faith*—something *practical* to live by, which automatically keeps us on our course. The mystery of life somehow loses its density *if we retain our spark of hope.*

All of my life since childhood I have held Shakespeare in constant companionship. Aside from the Bible—which is entirely apart from all other books—Shakespeare has no equal. My father, partly from his love for the great poet, and partly for the purpose of aiding me to memorize accurately, taught me to recite Shakespeare before I was old enough to know the meaning of the words. I remembered them, however, and in later years I grew to know their full significance. Then I became an ardent follower of the Master Philosopher, than whom no greater interpreter of human emotions ever lived. In the matter of sage advice there has never been his equal. In *"Hamlet"* we find the wonderful words of admonition from *Polonius* in his farewell speech to his son *Laertes*—as good today as four hundred years ago, and they will continue to be so until the end of time.

It matters not how familiar we may be with these lines it is no waste of time to read them over again once in awhile. They seem to fit the *practical side of life* perfectly. If we have any complaint by reason of their brusqueness we have only to temper our interpretation according to our own sense of justice. In other words if we wanted to loan a "ten-spot" now and then we would just go ahead and do it—meanwhile, to save you the trouble of looking up these lines, here they are in "Laugh and Live"—

And these few precepts in thy memory
See thou charácter—Give thy thoughts no
   tongue,
Nor any unproportioned thought his act.
Be thou familiar, but by no means vulgar.
The friends thou hast, and their adoption tried,
Grapple them to thy soul with hoops of steel;
But do not dull thy palm with entertainment
Of each new-hatch'd, unfledged comrade. Be-
   ware
Of entrance to a quarrel: but, being in,
Bear't that the opposed may beware of thee.
Give every man thine ear, but few thy voice:
Take each man's censure, but reserve thy judg-
   ment.
Costly thy habit as thy purse can buy,
But not express'd in fancy; rich, not gaudy:
For the apparel oft proclaims the man;
And they in France of the best rank and station
Are of a most select and generous sheaf in that.
Neither a borrower nor a lender be;
For loan oft loses both itself and friend,
And borrowing dulls the edge of husbandry,
This above all—*to thine ownself be true;*
And it must follow, as the night the day,
Thou canst not then be false to any man.

"Wedlock in Time"—The Fairbanks' Family

The time has come to close this little book. It has been a great pleasure to write it and a greater pleasure to hope that it will be received in the same spirit it has been written. These are busy days for all of us. We go in a gallop most of the time, but there comes the quiet hour when we must sit still and "take stock." I know this from the letters that come to me asking my opinion on all sorts of subjects. People believe I am happy because my laughing pictures seem to denote this fact—*and it is a fact!* In the foregoing chapters I have told why. If, in the telling I shall have been instrumental in adding to *the world's store of happiness* I shall ever thank my "lucky stars."

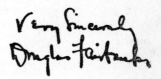

A "CLOSE-UP" OF
DOUGLAS FAIRBANKS

by

George Creel

Reprinted from Everybody's Magazine by Permission of

The Ridgway Company
New York.

CHAPTER XX

Young Mr. Douglas Fairbanks, star alike in both the "speakies" and the "movies," is well worth a story. He is what every American might be, ought to be, and frequently is *not*. More than any other that comes to mind, he is possessed of the indomitable optimism that gives purpose, "punch," and color to any life, no matter what the odds.

He holds the world's record for the standing broad grin. There isn't a minute of the day that fails to find him glad that he's alive. Nobody ever saw him with a "grouch," or suffering from an attack of the "blues." Nobody ever heard him mention "hard luck" in connection with one of his failures. The worse the breaks of the game, the gloomier the outlook, the wider his grin. He has made cheerfulness a habit, and

163

it has paid him in courage, in bubbling energy, and buoyant resolve.

We are a young nation and a great nation. Judging from the promise of the morning, there is nothing that may not be asked of America's noon. A land of abundance, with not an evil that may not be banished, and yet there is more whining in it than in any other country on the face of the globe. If we are to die, "Nibbled to Death by Ducks" may well be put on the tombstone. Little things are permitted to bring about paroxysms of peevishness. Even our pleasures have come to be taken sadly. We are irritable at picnics, snarly at clambakes, and bored to death at dinners.

The Government ought to hire Douglas Fairbanks, and send him over the country as an agent of the Bureau of Grins. Have him start work in Boston, and then rush him by special train to Philadelphia. If the wealth of the United States increased $41,000,000,000 during the last three peevish, whining years, think what would happen if we learned the art of joyousness and gained the strength that comes from good humor and optimism!

"Doug" Fairbanks—now that he is in the "movies" we don't have to be formal—is the living, breathing proof of the value of a grin. His rise from obscurity to fame, from poverty to wealth, has no larger foundation than his ever-ready willingness to let the whole world see every tooth in his head.

Good looks? Artistry? Bosh! The Fairbanks features were evidently picked out by a utilitarian mother who preferred use to ornament; and as for his acting, critics of the drama, imbued with the traditions of Booth and Barrett, have been known to sob like children after witnessing a Fairbanks performance.

It is the joyousness of the man that gets him over. It's the 100 per cent. *interest* that he takes in everything he goes at that lies at the back of his success. He does nothing by halves, is never indifferent, never lackadaisical.

At various stages in his brief career he has been a Shakespearean actor, Wall Street clerk,

hay steward on a cattle-boat, vagabond, and
business man, knowing poverty, hunger, and dis-
comfort at times, but never, *never* losing the
grin. Things began to move for him when he
left a Denver high school back in 1900 for the
purpose of entering college. As he says, "A man
can't be too careful about college."

He started for Princeton, but met a youth on
the train who was going to Harvard. He took
a special course at Cambridge—just what it was
he can't remember—but at the end of the year
it was hinted to him that circus life was more
suited to his talents, particularly one with three
rings.

A friend, however, suggested the theatre, and
gave him a card to Frederick Warde, the trage-
dian. Mr. Warde fell for the Fairbanks grin,
and as a first part assigned him the rôle of
François, the lackey, in "Richelieu." What he
lacked in experience he made up for in activity
and unflagging merriment. It got to be so that
Warde was almost afraid to touch the bell, for
he never knew whether the amazing *François*

would enter through the door or come down from the ceiling.

After the company had done its worst to "Richelieu," it changed to Shakespearean repertoire, and for one year young Fairbanks engaged in what Mr. Warde was pleased to term a "catch-as-catch-can bout with the immortal Bard." When friends of Shakespeare finally protested in the name of humanity, the strenuous Douglas accepted an engagement with Herbert Kelcey and Effie Shannon in "Her Lord and Master."

Five months went by before the two stars broke under the strain, and by that time news had come to Mr. Fairbanks that Wall Street was Easy Money's other name. Armed with his grin, he marched into the office of De Coppet & Doremus, and when the manager came out of his trance Shakespeare's worst enemy was holding down the job of order man.

"The name Coppet appealed to me," he explains.

He is still remembered in that office, fondly

but fearfully. He did his work well enough; in fact, there are those who insist that he invented scientific management.

"How about that?" I asked him, for it puzzled me.

"Well, you see, it was this way: For five days in a week I would say, 'Quite so' to my assistant, no matter what he suggested. On Saturday I would dash into the manager's office, wag my head, knit my brow, and exclaim, 'What we need around here is *efficiency.*' And once I urged the purchase of a time-clock."

The way he filled his spare time was what bothered. What with his tumbling tricks, boxing, wrestling, leap-frog over chairs, and other small gaieties, he mussed up routine to a certain extent. But he was *not* discharged. At a point where the firm was just one jump ahead of nervous prostration, along came "Jack" Beardsley and "Little" Owen, two husky football players with a desire to see life without the safety clutch.

The three approached the officials of a cattle-steamship, and by persistent claims to the effect that they "had a way" with dumb animals, got jobs as hay stewards.

"We found the cows very nice," comments Mr. Fairbanks. "No one can get me to say a word against them. But those stokers! And those other stable-maids! Pow! We had to fight 'em from one end of the voyage to the other, and it got so that I bit myself in my sleep. The three of us got eight shillings apiece when we landed at Liverpool, and tickets back, but there were several little things about Europe that bothered us, and we thought we'd see what the trouble was."

They "hoboed" it through England, France, and Belgium, working at any old job until they gathered money enough to move along, whether it was carrying water to English navvies or unloading paving-blocks from a Seine boat. After three joyous months, they felt the call of the cattle, and came home on another steamer.

Back on his native heath, young Fairbanks took a shot from the hip at law, but missed. Then he got a job in a machine-manufacturing plant, but one day he found that his carelessness had permitted fifty dollars to accumulate, and he breezed down to Cuba and Yucatan to see what openings there were for capital. Back from that tramping trip, he figured that since he had not annoyed the stage for some time it certainly owed him something.

His return to the drama took place in "The Rose of Plymouth Town," a play in which Miss Minnie Duprée was the star. Meeting Miss Duprée, I asked her what sort of an actor Fairbanks was in those days.

"Well," she said judiciously, "I think that he was about the nicest case of St. Vitus' dance that ever came under my notice."

William A. Brady got him next. Mr. Brady is quite a dynamo himself, and there was also a time in his life when he managed James J. Corbett. The two fell into each other's arms with a cry of joy, and for seven years they touched off dramatic explosions that strewed fat actors all over the landscape and tore miles of scenery into ribbons.

"Some boy!" was Mr. Brady's tribute. "Put him in a death scene, and he'd find a way to break the furniture."

There was never a part that "Doug" Fairbanks lay down on. To every rôle he brought joy and interest and enthusiasm, and the night came inevitably that saw his name in electric letters.

It is not claimed that his work as a star "elevated" the drama, but it may safely be claimed that he never appeared in any play that was not wholesome, stimulating, and helpful.

Nothing was more natural than that the movies should seek such an actor, and they set the trap with attractive bait.

"Come over to us," they said, "and we'll let you do anything you want. Outside of poison gas and actual murder, the sky's the limit."

Without even waiting to kick off his shoes, "Doug" Fairbanks made a dive.

The movie magnates got what they wanted, and Fairbanks got what he wanted. For the first time in his life he was able to "let go" with all the force of his dynamic individuality, and he took full advantage of the opportunity.

In "The Lamb," his first adventure before the camera, he let a rattlesnake crawl over him, tackled a mountain lion, jiu-jitsued a bunch of Yaqui Indians until they bellowed, and operated a machine-gun.

In "His Picture in the Papers," he was called upon to run an automobile over a cliff, engage in a grueling six-round go with a professional pugilist, jump off an Atlantic liner and swim to the distant shore, mix it up in a furious battle royal with a half dozen husky gunmen, leap twice from swiftly moving trains, and also to resist arrest by a squad of Jess Willards dressed up in police uniforms.

"The Half-Breed" carried him out to California, and, among other things, threw him into the heart of a forest fire that had been carefully kindled in the redwood groves of Calaveras County. Amid a rain of burning pine tufts, and with great branches falling to the ground all around him, "Douggie" was required to dash in and save the gallant sheriff from turning into a cinder. Hair and eyelashes grew out again, however, his blisters healed, and in a few days he was as good as new.

"The Habit of Happiness" was rich in stunts that would have made even Battling Nelson turn to tatting with a sigh of relief. Five gangsters, sicked on to their work by the villain, waylaid our hero on the stairs, and in the rough-and-tumble that followed, it was his duty to beat each and every one of them into a state of coma. He performed his task so conscientiously that his hands were swollen for a week, not to mention his eyes and nose. As for the five extra men who posed as the gangsters, all came to the conclusion that dock-walloping was far less strenuous than art, and went back to their former jobs.

"The Good Bad Man" was a Western picture that contained a thrill to every foot of film. Our hero galloped over mountains, jumping from crag to crag, held up an express train single-handed in order to capture the conductor's ticket-punch, grappled with gigantic desperadoes every few minutes, shot up a saloon, and was dragged around for quite a while at the end of a lynching party's rope.

"Reggie Mixes In" was one joyous round of assault and battery from beginning to end. Happening to fall in love with a dancer in a Bowery cabaret, *Reggie* puts family and fortune behind him and takes a job as "bouncer" so as to be near his lady-love. Aside from his regular duties, he is required to work overtime on account of the hatred of a gang-leader who also loves the girl. Five scoundrels jump *Reggie,* and, after manhandling four, he drops from a second-story window to the neck of the fifth, and chokes him with hands and legs. After which he carries the senseless wretch down the street, and gaily flicks him, as it were, through a window at the villain's feet. As a tasty little finish, *Reggie* and his rival lock themselves in an empty room, and engage in a contest governed by packing-house rules.

Three days after the combat, by the way, the company heads were pleased to announce that

White Studio

Here's Hoping!

both men were out of danger unless blood-poi-
soning set in.

"The Mystery of the Leaping Fish" was what
is known as a "water picture," and "Doug," as a
comedy detective, was compelled to make a human submarine of himself, not to mention several
duels in the dark with Japanese thugs and opium
smugglers.

"Another day of it," he grinned, "and I'd have
grown *fins*."

"Manhattan Madness" was really nothing
more than St. Vitus's dance set to ragtime. Our
hero climbed up eaves-pipes, plunged through
trap-doors down into dungeons, jumped from
the roof of a house into a tree, kicked his way in
and out of secret closets, and engaged in hair-
raising combats with desperate villains every few
minutes.

It is not only the case that "Doug" Fairbanks
made good with the movie fans. What is more
to the point, he made good with the "bunch" itself. In nine cases out of ten, the "legitimate"
star, going over into pictures, evades and avoids

the "rough stuff." To some humble, hardy "double" is assigned the actual work of falling off the cliff, riding at full speed across granite hedges, taking a good hard punch in the nose, or plunging from the top of the burning building.

Many an honest cowpuncher, taking his girl to the show with him to let her see what a daredevil he is, has died the death upon discovering that he was merely "doubling" for some coweyed hero who lacked the nerve to do the stunt himself.

"Doug" Fairbanks is one of the few movie heroes who have never had a "double." He asks no man to do that which he is afraid to do himself. No fall is too hard for him, no fight too furious, no ride too dangerous. There is not a single one of his pictures in which he hasn't taken a chance of breaking his neck or his bones; but, as one bronco-buster observed, "He jes' licks his lips an' asks for more."

To be sure, few actors have brought such super-physical equipment to the strenuous work of the movies. Fairbanks, in addition to being blessed with a strong, lithe body, has developed it by expert devotion to every form of athletic sport. He swims well, is a crack boxer, a good polo player, a splendid wrestler, a skilful acrobat, a fast runner, and an absolutely fearless rider.

There is never a picture during the progress of which he does not interpolate some sudden bit of business as the result of his quick wit and dynamic enthusiasm. In one play, for instance, he was supposed to enter a house at sight of his sweetheart beckoning to him from an upper window. As he passed up the steps, however, his roving eye caught sight of the porch railing, a window-ledge, and a balcony, and in a flash he was scaling the façade of the house like any cat.

In another play he was trapped on the roof of a country home. Suddenly Fairbanks, disregarding the plan of retreat indicated by the author, gave a wild leap into a near-by maple, managed to catch a bough, and proceeded to the ground in a series of convulsive falls that gave the director heart-failure.

During "The Half-Breed" picture, some of the action took place about a fallen redwood that had its great roots fully twenty feet into the air.

"Climb up on top of those roots, Doug," yelled the director.

Instead of that, "Douggie" went up to a young sapling that grew at the base of the fallen tree. Bending it down to the ground, as an archer bends his bow, he gave a sudden spring, and let the tough birch catapult him to the highest root.

"What do you want me to do now?" he grinned.

"Come back the same way," grinned the director.

Most "legitimate" actors—the valuation is their own—find the movies rather dull. Time hangs very heavily upon their hands. As one remarked to me in tones that were thick with a divine despair: "There's absolutely nothing for a chap to do. In lots of the God-forsaken holes they drag you to, there isn't even a hotel. No companionship, no diversion of any kind, and oftentimes no *bathtubs*."

Douglas Fairbanks enters no such complaint. He draws upon the energy and interest that ought to be in every human being, and when entertainment is not in sight, he goes after it. When they were making "The Half-Breed" pictures in the Carquinez woods of Northern California, he was never seen around the camp except when actually needed by the camera man. Upon his return from these absences, it was noticed that his hands were usually bleeding, and his clothing stained and torn.

"What in the name of mischief have you been doing now?" the director demanded on a day when Fairbanks's wardrobe was almost a total loss.

"Trappin'," chirped the star.

Beating about the woods, Bret Harte in hand, he had managed to discover an old woodsman who still held to the ancient industries of his youth. The trapper's specialty was "bob cats," and the bleeding hands and torn clothes came from "Doug's" earnest efforts to handle the "varmints" just as his venerable preceptor handled them. Out of the experience, at least, he brought an intimate knowledge of field, forest, and stream, for over the fire and in their walks he had pumped the old man dry.

In the same way he made "The Good Bad Man" hand him over everything of value that frontier life contained. The picture was taken out in the Mohave desert; for the making of it the director had scoured the West for riders and ropers and cowboys of the old school. "He men" —every one of them, and for a time they looked with dislike and suspicion upon the "star," but when they saw that Fairbanks did not ask for any "double," and took the hardest tumble with a grin, they received him into their fellowship with a heartfelt yell.

Dull in the Mohave desert? Why, he had to sit up nights to keep even with his engagements. From one man he learned bronco-busting, from another fancy roping, and from others all that there is to know about horses, cattle, mountain, and plain. And around the camp-fires he got stories of the winning of the West such as never found their way into histories.

When one picture called for jiu-jitsu work, he didn't rest satisfied with learning just enough to "get by." Every spare moment found him in a clinch with the Japanese expert, mastering every secret, perfecting himself in every hold. Same way with boxing. When no pugilists came handy, he put on the gloves with anyone willing to take chances on a black eye, keeping at it until today they have to hire professionals when he figures in a movie fight.

When they made a "water" picture he never stopped until he could duplicate every trick known to the "professor" who drilled the extra men. He took advantage of a biplane flight to make friends with the aeronaut, and by the time the picture was done, he was as good a driver as the expert.

No matter where he is, or what the job, he

finds something of interest because he goes upon the theory that every minute is meant to be *lived*. Maroon him at a cross-roads, with five hours until train time, and he'd have the operator's first name in ten minutes and be learning the Morse alphabet, after which he would rush up to his new friend's house to see the babies or to pass judgment on a Holstein calf or a Black Minorca brood.

It is the tremendously human quality, more than anything else, that gets him across. People like him because he likes them. He attracts interest because he takes interest. Talk with any of the big men in the motion-picture industry, that is, those with brains and education, and they will tell you that *personality* counts more in pictures than it does on the stage.

H. E. Aitken, president of the Triangle Film Corporation, said to me: "The screen is *intimate*. The camera brings the actor right into your lap. In the speaking drama, make-up and footlights change and hide, but not the least flicker of expression is lost in the picture. It's a test of real-

© Lumiere

A Close-Up

ness, and it takes a real man or a real woman to stand it. Art isn't the thing at all, nor do looks count for half as much as people suppose. It's what's back of the art and the looks that makes the hit, and if they haven't got *something,* the artist and the beauty don't last long. We picked Douglas Fairbanks as a likely film star, not on account of his stunts, as the majority think, but because of the splendid humanness that fairly oozed out of him."

When he isn't before the camera, or fooling with an airship or a motor, or playing with children, or "gettin' acquainted" with a tramp or a trapper, or practising stunts with a rope or a horse, young Mr. Fairbanks fills in his spare time writing scenarios. As everyone knows, the motion-picture drama has been a tawdry thing for the most part—either a rehash of old stage plays, novels, and short stories, or else mediocre "originalities" that epitomized banality. Young Mr. Fairbanks dissented from the established custom from the very start.

"It's all wrong," he declared. "We've got to

stand on our own feet. Develop your own dramatists!"

Practically every play in which he has appeared sprang from his personal suggestion, and in many of them he has collaborated with the scenario writer. The three things that he demands are Action, Wholesomeness, and Sentiment that rings true.

Never make the mistake of thinking that Douglas Fairbanks starts and finishes with mere good humor and physical exuberance. There is more to him than his grin, for his mind is as strong and vigorous as his body. He reads and thinks, and behind his smile is a quick and eager sympathy that takes account of the sadnesses of life as well as its promises.

"The Habit of Happiness" was very much his own idea, and in it he took occasion to show a midnight bread-line, the misery of the slums, and various forms of social injustice. It isn't that he thinks himself called to uplift and reform, but, as he expresses it, "Every little bit helps."

In the last talk that I had with him, he was

enthusiastic over the future of the movies as a world force. He speaks in ideas rather than words, for when he feels that he has indicated the thought he never troubles to finish the particular sentence.

"Pictures are like music," he declared. "They speak a universal language. Great industry— just in its infancy—before long films will pass from one country to another—internationalism. Why not? Love, hate, grief, ambition, laughter —they belong to one race as much as another— all peoples understand them. It's hard to hate people after you know them. Pictures will let us know each other. They'll break down the hard national lines that now make for war and suspicion."

Other things followed, for we discussed everything from cabbages to kings, and then I plumped the question at him that I had been waiting to ask from the first.

"How do you like the movies as compared to the speaking drama? Come now, cross your heart and hope to die. When the night comes down and the lights go up, isn't there a blue minute now and then?"

"Surest thing you know," he grinned. "It isn't because there's such a radical difference between the 'talkies' and the movies, however." [He refers to musical comedy as the "scream-ies."] "The play in the theatre is largely a matter of pantomime, you know. Dialogue is employed to advance the actual plot only when it is impossible or impracticable to do it with dumb show. And when I think of some of the lines I've been called upon to spout, I can't say that I regret the movies' lack of dialogue.

"What does hurt, though," he admitted, "is the absence of *response*. I don't mean applause, but the something that comes up over the foot-lights to you from the audience, the big some-thing that tells you instantly whether you have hit it or missed, whether you are ringing true or false. You don't get that in the pictures. Your audience is the director, and you know that it will be weeks or months before your work is going to get its test.

"But in everything else, the movie has the talkie skinned a mile. Instead of mouthing somebody else's words, you are doing the thing yourself. There's action, and life—one day you are in the forest, the next in the desert, the next on the sea."

"Nonsense!" I exclaimed. "I understand that it's all done in a studio."

"I had the idea myself," he laughed. "But no more. When I was in the 'talkies,' I used to hear a lot about realism. Father must wash in a real basin with real water and real soap. There had to be two hens at least in every barnyard scene, and when Lottie came home from the cruel city, she had to have a real baby in her arms. Lordy, I never knew what realism was until I struck the movies. They've gone crazy over it.

" 'The Half-Breed,' you know, was adapted from one of Bret Harte's stories, and nothing would do the director but a trip up to the Carquinez woods in northern California. A forest fire figured in one of the scenes, but I never thought much about it until I saw them bringing up some chemical engines, hose reels, and five or six fire-brigades.

" 'What's the idea?' I asked.

" 'To keep the flames from spreading,' they told me.

"And let me tell you, it was *some* fire. After I got out of it I felt like a shave from a Mexican barber."

"What effect is the movie going to have on the speaking drama?" was my next question.

"Look at the effect it's had already," he said. "Shaw is the only playwright clever enough to write dialogue that will hold any number of people in the theatre. The motion picture has made the public demand *action*. It has changed the plot and progress of the drama completely."

"Do you think that a good thing? Doesn't it mean the substitution of feeling for thinking?"

"Well," he answered slowly, "the world goes forward through the heart rather than through the head. Happiness, to my mind, is emotional, not mental. And the movie *has* brought happiness to millions whose lives were formerly drab and sordid. I love to go into these little halls in out-of-the-way places, and see the men, women, and children packed there of an evening. Theatrical companies never reached the villages, and the men had no place but the saloon, the women no place but the kitchen or the front porch. The camera has brought the world to their doors, and life is richer, happier, and better for it."

Take him as he stands, and Douglas Fairbanks comes close to being the "real thing." Men like him as well as women, and, best proof of all, the "kids" adore him. On a recent visit to Denver, his old home town, youngsters followed him in droves, clamoring for a chance to "feel his muscle." The mayor, no less, had him address a public meeting, the feature of which, by the way, was this piped inquiry from the gallery:

"Say, Doug, can youse whip William Farnum?"

And let no one quarrel with this popularity. It is a good sign, a healthful sign, a token that the blood of America still runs warm and red, and that chalk has not yet softened our bones.

Date Due
